FUNDAMENTAL COMMUNICATION ENGLISH

Level 1

KMU CE 1 Committee:

NA-GYUNG SOHN

WOO-HYUNG KIM

JON DARREN HOLMES

ROBERT CHARLES KERR

PHILIP BRADY WESTON HELMER

RODNEY ALAN HAMBEL

SHANNON PATRICK BERRY

NATIONAL GEOGRAPHIC LEARNING

Australia • Brazil • Mexico • Singapore • United Kingdom • United States

SCOPE & SEQUENCE

UNIT 1 PEOPLE p. 2

Unit / Lesson	Video	Vocabulary	Listening
LESSON **A** Getting to know you	World's Biggest Melting Pot	Personal information *city, email address, hometown, last name*	Where is he from? Make predictions Listen for details
LESSON **B** Appearance		Physical descriptions *young, tall, thin, blue eyes, long hair*	What does he look like? Use background knowledge Listen for gist Listen for details

UNIT 2 ACTIVITIES p. 18

Unit / Lesson	Video	Vocabulary	Listening
LESSON **A** What are you doing?	Day in the Life of a College Student	Things we do *listen (to music), study (for a test)*	People talk about activities Make predictions Listen for gist and details
LESSON **B** At school		School subjects and majors *business, history, science*	Taking classes Make predictions Distinguish speakers Listen for details

UNIT 3 SHOPPING p. 34

Unit / Lesson	Video	Vocabulary	Listening
LESSON **A** At the market	Field of Greens	What foods are in your kitchen? *chicken, fish, eggs*	Shopping list Use background knowledge Listen for gist Listen for details
LESSON **B** Let's go shopping!		Shopping *credit card, on sale, a mall*	Going to the store Listen for gist Listen for details

Review Units 1–3 p. 50

UNIT 4 VACATION p. 52

Unit / Lesson	Video	Vocabulary	Listening
LESSON **A** Weather	Imersão (Immersion)	Weather words *hot, foggy, raining*	A weather forecast Listen for details
LESSON **B** Traveling		When you travel *get a passport, go sightseeing*	On vacation Infer information Listen for gist Listen for context Make predictions; Listen for details

UNIT 5 FOOD p. 68

Unit / Lesson	Video	Vocabulary	Listening
LESSON **A** What's on the menu?	At the Covered Market	Foods and drinks *coffee, chicken, sandwich*	Ordering food; talking about meals Listen for details
LESSON **B** Eating right		Tips for being a healthy eater *healthy, energy, junk food*	Make a smoothie Make and check predictions Listen for details Listen for sequence

UNIT 6 RELATIONSHIPS p. 84

Unit / Lesson	Video	Vocabulary	Listening
LESSON **A** Family	Megafamily	Family members *father, mother, sister, brother*	Extended family Make predictions Listen for details
LESSON **B** Marriage		Relationships *single, married, divorced*	Modern marriage Listen for gist Listen for details

Review Units 4–6 p. 100

Grammar	Pronunciation	Speaking	Reading	Writing	Communication
The simple present tense Describing appearance using *be / have*	Question intonation review	Introducing yourself; Asking about occupations	Celebrity Doubles Skim for gist Scan for details	Describe a classmate	Ask questions to find classmates with various interests Describe a person
The present continuous tense: affirmative and negative statements The present continuous tense: extended time	Question intonation	Greeting people and asking how they are	Study Abroad Identify main ideas Infer meaning Find key details	Answer interview questions	Play charades Act out and identify actions A student interview Interview classmates
Count and noncount nouns Quantifiers with affirmative and negative statements	Syllables	Talking about things you need	On Sale in Seoul Make predictions Identify main ideas Scan for details	Write about your favorite place to shop	Choose items to take on an island survival trip List items a person needs and say where to buy them
Connecting ideas with *but*, *or*, and *so* Possessive adjectives; possessive pronouns; *belong to*	Stress in multi-syllable words	Giving advice	How to Pack for Your Next Trip Understand the gist Make predictions Identify main ideas Scan for details	Write about a traveling experience	Ask questions and pick a vacation destination for a partner Ask questions about a partner's vacation
Affirmative and negative statements *Yes / No* questions and short answers	*And*, *or*	Talking about likes and dislikes	Two Powerful Health Foods Scan for information Read for details	Write about a favorite food	Plan a dinner party Create a seating chart for guests according to personal information Talk about your favorite food Express agreement and disagreement
Possessive nouns *Have got*	Possessive nouns: *'s*	Asking and answering questions about family	Time to Get Married? Make predictions Read for details	Write about your family	Famous families Research and talk about family members Take a relationship survey Take a survey and explain answers Discuss results

SCOPE & SEQUENCE

UNIT 7 TIME p. 102

Unit / Lesson	Video	Vocabulary	Listening
LESSON **A** My routine LESSON **B** Have a good weekend	Late for Work	**Times and daily routines** *What time is it?, It's 9:15; wake up, take a shower, get dressed* **Weekend activities** *go to the movies, go for a walk*	**What are your plans?** Listen for gist Listen for details **Days off** Listen for details

UNIT 8 CITY LIFE p. 118

Unit / Lesson	Video	Vocabulary	Listening
LESSON **A** My neighborhood LESSON **B** Big cities	My City: Stockholm	**Places in a neighborhood** *train station, coffee shop* **What's your city like?** *rush hour, pollution*	**Is this your neighborhood?** Listen for details Make and check predictions **A tourism ad** Listen for context Listen for details

UNIT 9 ALL ABOUT YOU p. 134

Unit / Lesson	Video	Vocabulary	Listening
LESSON **A** Sports LESSON **B** Personality	Yoga in Schools	**Sports and activities** *swimming, tennis, surfing* **Personality traits** *organized, messy, talkative, reserved*	**From physician to beach bum** Use visual cues Make predictions Listen for gist and details **Personality types** Use visual cues Infer Listen for gist and details

Review Units 7–9 p. 150

UNIT 10 HEALTH p. 152

Unit / Lesson	Video	Vocabulary	Listening
LESSON **A** The body LESSON **B** Stress	Centenarian's Guide to Longevity	**Our bodies** *arm, back, shoulder, head* **I'm stressed.** *deal with, reduce, take time*	**There's a stranger in my house!** Make predictions Listen for details **Now I'm full of energy!** Listen for gist Listen for details Draw conclusions

UNIT 11 JOBS p. 168

Unit / Lesson	Video	Vocabulary	Listening
LESSON **A** What do you do? LESSON **B** Getting a job	Career Day	**Jobs** *doctor, programmer, lawyer, nurse* **Work goals** *internship, experience, make money*	**A part-time job** Listen for details Draw conclusions **Summer jobs** Make predictions Listen for details Listen for a speaker's attitude

UNIT 12 AT THE MOVIES p. 184

Unit / Lesson	Video	Vocabulary	Listening
LESSON **A** Types of movies LESSON **B** Movie reviews	Spider-Man in Real Life	**Types of movies** *action (movie), drama, horror film* **Review a movie!** *hilarious, depressing, sweet, scary*	**Movie preferences** Make predictions Check predictions Listen for details **Deciding what to watch** Listen for a speaker's opinion Listen for details

Review Units 10–12 p. 200

Grammar	Pronunciation	Speaking	Reading	Writing	Communication
Prepositions of time: in, on, at, from... to Simple present *Wh-* questions	Numbers: stress; *-ty* and *-teen*	Making suggestions	What Kind of Weekend Person Are You? Make predictions Check predictions Read for specific information	Make plans	Make a schedule and find time to meet with classmates Interview classmates about weekend activities
Prepositions of place Questions and answers with *How much / How many*	Stress in compound noun phrases	Asking for and giving directions	City Living Make predictions Read for details	Write an ad to promote a city	Use logic to solve a crime Present a brochure to the class
Verb + infinitive; verb + noun *How often…?* frequency expressions	Reduced *to*	Inviting and offering with *Do you want*	Life Style Use background knowledge Make predictions Scan for information Read for details	Describe your personality	Guess a classmate's identity from survey answers Take a personality quiz and talk about the results
Imperatives *When* clauses	Vowel length with voiced and voiceless consonants	Talking about health problems	How to Deal with Study Stress Make predictions Read for main ideas Infer meaning Understand a writer's opinion	Write about a stressful situation and give advice	Make and present a poster to increase health awareness Role-play different stressful situations
Questions with *like* Talking about ability with *can / can't*	Reduced words	Talking about jobs	Internet Entrepreneur Michelle Phan Make predictions Read for details Skim for information	Write about personal work goals	Exchange business cards and personal information Interview a partner about his or her job skills
The present continuous as future *-ed / -ing* adjectives	Syllable stress	Taking and leaving a message	A Movie Remake Use background knowledge Make predictions Check predictions Read for details	Write about a movie you like	Create a new movie and make a poster Talk about favorite movies

Language Summaries p. 204 · Grammar Notes p. 215

1 PEOPLE

Look at the photo. Answer the questions.

1 What kinds of people do you see?

2 What are the people doing?

3 What are they thinking about?

UNIT GOALS

1 Ask questions to get basic personal information

2 Introduce yourself

3 Talk about where you come from and what you do

4 Describe a person's appearance

People look at an art exhibition in Santiago de Compostela, Spain.

LESSON A GETTING TO KNOW YOU

People on a busy street in New York City

1 VIDEO World's Biggest Melting Pot

A Look at the photo of New York City. What do you notice about it? Tell a partner.

B Watch the video. Circle your answers.

1. Welcome to Brooklyn / Queens New York.
2. Almost half the people here were born in New York / another country.
3. They speak almost 50 / 150 languages.

half = 50%

C Watch the video again. Complete the sentences.

1. "I'm from Madras, the southern part of India. My __________ live there and my grandparents live there."
2. "My mom's from South Korea and on my father's side I am __________, Irish, English..."
3. "So you have Eastern Europeans. You have Hispanics. You have __________. You have Arabic. I like that."

D Is your city similar to or different from this neighborhood? Use your answers in **B** and **C** to explain to a partner.

2 VOCABULARY

A Look at Silvia's LinkBook page. Do you have a page like this?

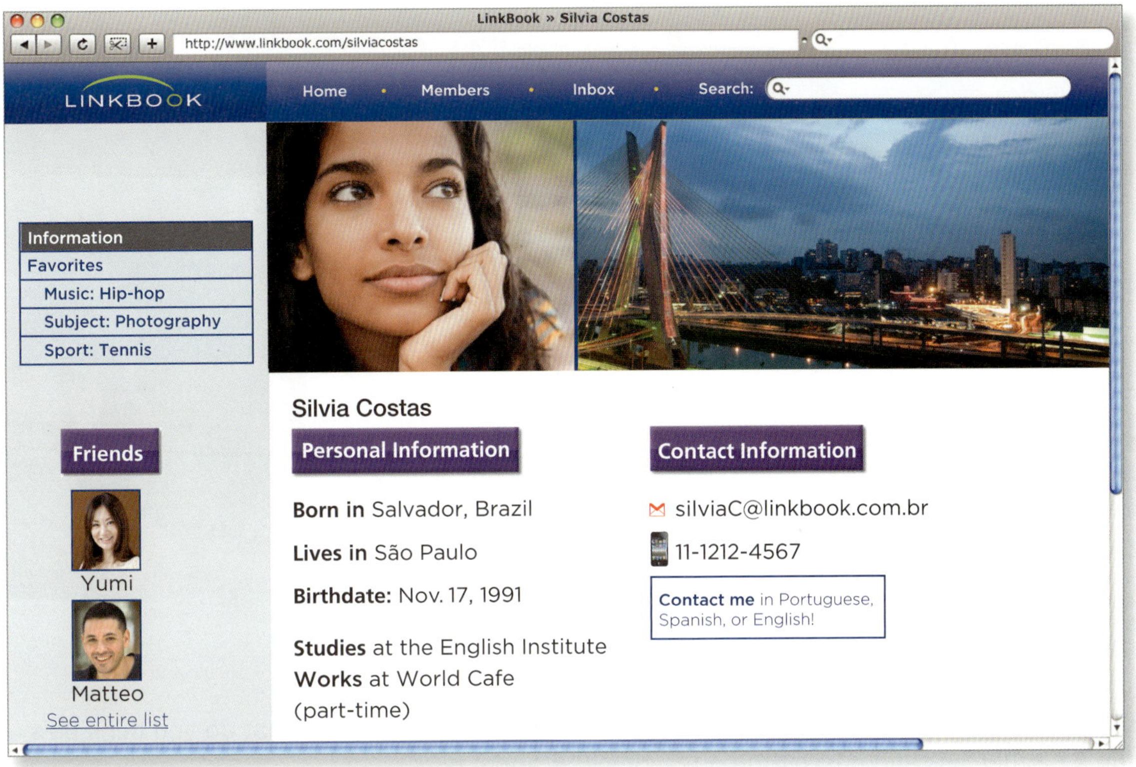

Saying email addresses

silviaC@linkbook .com.br = silvia C (at) linkbook (dot) com (dot) b-r

B Look at Silvia's web page. Complete the questions and answers with a partner. Use the words in the box.

born	**city**	**first name**	**hometown**	**job**	**last name**
phone	**email address**	**friends**	**interested in**	**languages**	**subject**

1. What's your ______________? (It's) Silvia.
2. What's your ______________? (It's) Costas.
3. Where were you born? I was ______________ in Salvador. It's my ______________.
4. Where do you live now? São Paulo. It's a fun ______________!
5. What do you do for fun? I'm in a band with my ______________, Yumi and Matteo.
6. What's your favorite ______________? I'm ______________ photography.
7. How many ______________ do you speak? Three. I speak Portuguese, Spanish, and English.
8. What's your ______________? (It's) silviaC@linkbook.com.br.
9. What's your ______________ number? (It's) 11-1212-4567.
10. What do you do? I'm a student, and I have a part-time ______________.

C Use the questions in **B** to interview your partner.

3 LISTENING

A **Pronunciation: Question intonation review.** Read these questions. Then listen and repeat. Make new questions by changing the words *he* and *his* to *you* and *your*. Ask and answer the questions with a partner. **Track 1**

1. Where's he from?
2. What's his hometown?
3. What does he do?
4. What are his interests?

B **Make predictions.** Look at the photo of Silvia's friend from LinkBook. What do you think he's like? With a partner, ask and answer the questions in **A** about him.

C **Listen for details.** Silvia and her friend are on her computer. Listen. Circle the best answers. **Track 2**

1. His name is ________. a. Lawrence b. Lars c. Larry
2. He speaks ________ languages. a. two b. three c. four
3. He's from ________. a. Switzerland b. England c. Sweden
4. His hometown is ________. a. Stockholm b. Visby c. Bern
5. He's a ________ student. a. business b. math c. science
6. He's interested in travel and ________. a. music b. languages c. movies

D In your notebook, complete the sentences in **C** about your best friend. Change pronouns if needed. Tell a partner about your friend.

E What are you interested in? Check the boxes. Then ask a partner about his or her answers.

I'm interested in...

- ☐ music.
- ☐ languages.
- ☐ travel.
- ☐ video games.
- ☐ sports.
- ☐ cooking.
- ☐ movies.
- ☐ your idea: ________

I like music and video games.

Really? I'm interested in music, too. What's your favorite kind of music?

4 SPEAKING

A Mariana and Danny live in the same apartment building. Listen. Are they meeting for the first time? How do you know? **Track 3**

MARIANA: Hi. My name is Mariana. I'm in apartment 201.
DANNY: Hi, Mariana. I'm Danny. I'm in 302. It's nice to meet you.
MARIANA: Nice to meet you, too.
DANNY: So, are you a student, Mariana?
MARIANA: Yeah, I study music at NYU.
DANNY: That's interesting.
MARIANA: What do you do, Danny?
DANNY: I'm a student at Hunter College. I also work in an art gallery.

B Practice the conversation with a partner. Then practice with *your* information.

SPEAKING STRATEGY

C Introduce yourself to four classmates. Then ask about their names and occupations. Complete the chart with their information. Use the Useful Expressions to help you.

Useful Expressions	
Introducing yourself	**Asking about occupations**
A: My name is Mariana. B: Hi, I'm Danny. (It's) Nice to meet you. A: (It's) Nice to meet you, too.	A: What do you do? B: I'm a music student.
Speaking tip	
When you are introducing yourself, *My name is...* and *I'm...* can both be used.	

Name	Occupation
Clara	student (studies art)
1.	
2.	
3.	
4.	

D Tell a partner about the classmates you talked to in **C**.

Clara is a student.
She studies art.

5 GRAMMAR

A Turn to page 215. Complete the exercise. Then do **B–E** below.

The Simple Present Tense		
	Questions	**Answers**
Yes / No* questions with *be	**Are** you a student? **Is** he a student?	Yes, I **am**. / No, I**'m** not. Yes, he **is**. / No, he**'s** not.
***Yes / No* questions with other verbs**	**Do** you **speak** English? **Does** she **speak** English?	Yes, I **do**. / No, I **don't**. Yes, she **does**. / No, she **doesn't**.
***Wh-* questions**	What do you do? What does she do?	I'm a student. She's a doctor.

B Steffi is writing about herself and her classmate. Read the sentences. Write the correct form of each verb.

Monika and Me

Monika (1. be) ___is___ my classmate. We (2. be) ________ different in many ways. I (3. be) ________ an only child. Monika (4. have) ________ two brothers and a sister. I (5. live) ________ with my family. Monika (6. live) ________ in her own apartment. We both go to Western University, but I (7. study) ________ English literature and Monika (8. study) ________ business. I (9. not have) ________ a job, but Monika (10. work) ________ part-time in a cafe. I (11. love) ________ dance music, but Monika (12. not like) ________ it. She (13. listen) ________ to rap. Monika and I (14. watch) ________ TV together on the weekends.

C Complete questions 1–4 with the correct form of *be* or *do*. Complete questions 5–8 with a *Wh-* question word. Take turns asking and answering the questions with a partner.

1. ________ Steffi and Monika different?
2. ________ Steffi an only child?
3. ________ Steffi study business?
4. ________ Monika and Steffi go to the same university?
5. ________ subject does Steffi study?
6. ________ does Monika work?
7. ________ does Steffi live with?
8. ________ does Monika live?

D Complete each sentence with an affirmative or negative verb in the box to make it true for you.

speak	have	study	like

1. I ________ a middle name.
2. I ________ my first name.
3. I ________ more than one language well.
4. I ________ on the weekend.
5. I ________ my hometown.
6. I ________ a favorite subject at school.

E How are you and your partner similar and different? Use the sentences in **D** to form questions. Ask follow-up questions.

Do you have a middle name?

Yes, I do.

What is it?

It's Victor.

6 COMMUNICATION

A For each item in the chart, ask the question until you find a person who answers *Yes*. Write his or her name. Then ask one follow-up question and write the extra information.

> **i** Follow-up questions are an important part of conversation. Make sure to ask a follow-up question related to what your partner already said. *Wh-* questions usually work better than *Yes / No* questions.

Find someone who...	Classmate's Name	Extra Information
1. has a part-time job.		
2. travels sometimes.		
3. likes listening to rap music.		
4. is a university student.		
5. plays soccer.		
6. has a sister.		
7. goes dancing on the weekends.		
8. knows his or her cell number in English.		
9. drives a car.		
10. eats breakfast every day.		
11. knows an email address in English.		
12. watches movies every week.		
13. speaks three languages.		
14. is an only child.		
15. your idea: ________		

Do you have a part-time job?

Yes, I do.

What do you do?

I work in a bookstore.

B Tell a classmate about the people in your chart.

LESSON B APPEARANCE

Use *be* with…	Use *have* with…
Age	**Eye color**
young	(dark) brown
in his / her teens*	blue
in his / her twenties*	green
elderly (80+)	
	Hairstyle
Weight	long ↔ short
skinny	straight ↔ curly
thin	wavy
slim**	spiky
average weight	
heavy	**Hair color**
	black
Height	(light / dark) brown
short	blond
average height	red
tall	gray
	Facial hair
	beard
	mustache

*teens (13–19), twenties (ages 20–29), thirties, forties

***Slim* means skinny / thin, but *slim* has a positive meaning.

1 VOCABULARY

A Complete the sentences about each person in the family photo. Use the words in the box. Then take turns telling a partner about each person.

1. Emilio is __in his fifties__ (age). He is __tall__ (height). He is __average weight__ (weight).
   He has __brown__ eyes. He has __short__, __gray__ hair.
2. Kathy is ____________ (age). She is ____________ (height). She is ____________ (weight).
   She has ____________ eyes. She has ____________, straight, ____________ hair.
3. Michael is ____________ (age). He is ____________ (height). He is ____________ (weight).
   He has ____________ eyes. He has ____________, ____________, ____________ hair.
4. Alexis and Ashley are ____________ (age). They are ____________ (height). They are ____________ (weight).
   They have ____________ eyes. They have ____________, wavy hair.

B Answer the questions with a partner.

1. Who does Michael look like? He **looks like** __his father__. They're both tall.
2. Who does Ashley look like? She **looks like** ____________. They both have red hair.
3. Who do you look like? I **look like** ____________. We're both... / We both have...

I look like my mom. We're both tall and slim, and we both have dark, curly hair.

2 LISTENING

A **Use background knowledge.** Look at the pictures below. Describe the man's appearance in each one. Tell a partner.

B **Listen for gist.** Read the sentence below. Then listen and complete it.

Emily is at the airport. She is ____ her uncle Tim. **Track 4**

a. traveling with   b. looking for   c. talking to   d. shopping for

C **Listen for details.** Now listen to the entire conversation. Circle the words that describe Uncle Tim before and now. Then check (✓) the correct picture of Uncle Tim now in **A**. **Track 5**

1. Uncle Tim before:

   short / tall   short hair / long hair   brown hair / blond hair

2. Uncle Tim now:

   short / tall   short hair / long hair   brown hair / blond hair

D Think about your appearance in the past. Is anything different now? Complete the sentences. Tell a partner.

In the past, I was ______________________________.

Now I am ______________________________.

In the past, I had ______________________________.

Now I have ______________________________.

In the past, I had short, brown hair. Now I have long, blond hair.

3 READING

A Look at the photo. Who are these people? What do they do? Tell a partner.

B **Skim for gist.** Read the passage. Then complete the sentence below.

The reading is mainly about ________.

a. the actor Daniel Radcliffe
b. people who look like celebrities
c. good-looking actors
d. famous people with a lot of money

C **Scan for details.** Quickly find and underline the answers to questions 1 and 2 in the reading.

1. How does Andrew Walker make money?
2. How do celebrity doubles make money?

D Answer the questions with a partner.

1. Look at the photo of the two men singing. Do they look alike? Why or why not?
2. Is being a celebrity double fun? Why or why not?
3. Do you (or someone you know) look like a famous person? Who? Explain.

CELEBRITY DOUBLES

Track 6

Actor Daniel Radcliffe

A group of teenagers is standing outside a shop in Manchester, England. Many of them have cameras and are looking in the shop window. They want to see celebrity Daniel Radcliffe. A man in the shop looks like Radcliffe. He has brown hair and Radcliffe's good looks. But the young man in the shop isn't the famous actor. He's Andrew Walker, a 22-year-old shop clerk.

Comedian Jimmy Fallon (right) and musician Bruce Springsteen perform together.

Walker isn't surprised by the teenagers. People often stop him on the street and want to take his picture. Walker is a clerk, but he also makes money as Radcliffe's double. Walker travels all over Europe as Daniel Radcliffe. It's an exciting life for the shop clerk from Manchester.

Today, many companies work with celebrity doubles. The most popular celebrity doubles look like famous athletes, pop singers, and actors. The companies pay doubles to go to parties and business meetings. Doubles are also on TV and in commercials.

Some celebrities even dress up as doubles. American talk show host Jimmy Fallon is famous for dressing up and performing as famous musicians. He looks and sounds just like them. Sometimes the real musicians even come on his show!

4 GRAMMAR

A Turn to page 216. Complete the exercises. Then do **B–D** below.

Describing Appearance			
Subject	***be / have***	**Adjective**	**Noun**
He	**is**	tall.	
		average	height / weight.
		young / in his teens.	
	has	blue	eyes.
		spiky, black	hair.

B Work with a partner. Practice the conversation. Can you guess the person? Check your answer on the bottom of the page.

A: I'm thinking of a famous person.
B: Is it a woman?
A: No, it's a man.
B: Is he British?
A: No, he's not. He's from Argentina.
B: Is he tall?
A: No, he's not. He's a little short.
B: Is he in his twenties?
A: Yes, I think he's in his late twenties.
B: Does he have long hair?
A: No, he doesn't.
B: Is he a soccer player?
A: Yes, he is.
B: I know! It's...

C Think of a famous person. Complete the notes below.

Name: ________ Hair: ________ Height: ________
Job: ________ Eyes: ________ Weight: ________
Nationality: ________ Age: ________

D Ask your partner seven questions. Try to guess his or her person. Then switch roles.

5 WRITING

A Read the paragraph on the right. Then write five or six sentences about a classmate's appearance on a separate piece of paper. Use the paragraph as a model. Don't write your classmate's name.

> My classmate is in his twenties. He's average height—he's about 172 centimeters. He has short, straight, brown hair. He has dark brown eyes (I think). He doesn't wear glasses.

B Exchange papers with a partner.

1. Are there any mistakes in your partner's writing? If yes, circle them.
2. Can you guess the person? Write his or her name on the paper.

Answer **B**: Lionel Messi

6 COMMUNICATION

A Work in a group of four. Each person chooses a photo above. Think about your answers to the questions below.

1. What does the person in your photo look like? Describe him or her.
2. In your opinion, is the person good-looking? Why or why not?

B Tell the group your answers in **A**. Do your partners agree with you? Why or why not?

I think he's very handsome.

He's OK. I don't like his beard or hairstyle.

Word Bank

Other words to describe appearance

Has...
a nice smile
a tattoo

Is...
pretty
handsome
good-looking

C Now find a photo of someone else online. Show it to your group. Then repeat **A** and **B**.

MEMO

NATIONAL GEOGRAPHIC LEARNING

KEIMYUNG UNIVERSITY

MEMO

2 ACTIVITIES

A woman looks at her phone on a crowded subway.

Look at the photo. Answer the questions.

1 Where are the people?

2 What is the woman doing?

3 What are three things you do every day?

UNIT GOALS

1 Describe what you're doing

2 Tell how you are feeling and ask how other people are feeling

3 Talk about school subjects and activities

4 Talk about long-term plans

LESSON A WHAT ARE YOU DOING?

A group of students sitting outside of a school building

1 VIDEO Day in the Life of a College Student

A Watch the video with the sound off. Where are these people? What do they do? Write three things.

____

____

____

B Watch the video again with the sound on. Check your answers.

C What are the people in the video doing? Tell a partner.

2 VOCABULARY

A What are these people doing? Match each sentence with a photo.

1. He's **doing** his homework and **studying** for a test.
2. He's **watching** TV.
3. He's **texting** a friend.
4. She's **exercising** and **listening** to music.
5. He's **talking** on the phone.
6. She's **eating** pizza and **drinking** soda.
7. They're **going** to school.
8. She's **shopping**.

B Cover up the sentences. Point to a person and ask your partner a question.

What's he doing?

He's doing his homework.

3 LISTENING

A **Pronunciation: Question intonation.** Read the dialog below. Practice it with a partner.

A: How are you[1] doing today?
B: Fine, thanks. How about you[2]?
A: I'm doing great.

[1] Sounds like *How're you*
[2] Sounds like *How 'bout you*

B **Pronunciation: Question intonation.** Listen and repeat. **Track 7**

C **Make predictions.** You will hear three conversations in **D**. Read the key words from each conversation. What are the people doing in each situation? Tell a partner what you think.

Conversation 1: *popular, expensive, buy*
Conversation 2: *park, running*
Conversation 3: *notebook, pen*

D **Listen for gist and details.** Listen to the conversations. What is each person doing? Circle the correct answer. **Track 8**

1. A B C
2. A B C
3. A B C

E Check your answers with a partner.

4 SPEAKING

A Listen to the conversation. Then answer the questions with a partner. Track 9

1. What is Shinja doing? What is Luis doing?
2. How is Shinja? How is Luis?

SHINJA: Hello?
LUIS: Hey, Shinja. It's Luis.
SHINJA: Hi, Luis. How are you doing?
LUIS: Fine. How about you?
SHINJA: So-so.
LUIS: Yeah? What's wrong?
SHINJA: I'm waiting for the bus. It's late!
LUIS: Sorry to hear that.
SHINJA: What are you doing, Luis?
LUIS: Not much. I'm watching TV.

B Practice the conversation in **A** with a partner.

SPEAKING STRATEGY

C Complete the dialogs below. Use the Useful Expressions to help you. Then practice the dialogs with a partner.

Useful Expressions	
Greeting people and asking how they are	
Positive ☺	A: Hi, Sara. How are you doing? B: Fine. / OK. / All right. / Not bad. How about you? A: I'm fine, thanks.
Negative ☹	A: Hi, Yuki. How's it going? B: So-so. / Not so good. A: Really? / Yeah? What's wrong? B: I'm waiting for the bus. It's late!

1. A: Hi, __________. How __________?
   B: __________ good.
   A: Really? __________?
   B: I'm studying for a test. It's hard!

2. A: Hi, __________. How __________?
   B: Fine. How __________?
   A: All __________. What __________?
   B: Not much. I'm reading a book.

D Ask four people in your class how they are doing today.

5 GRAMMAR

A Turn to page 217. Complete the exercise. Then do **B** and **C** below.

<table>
<tr><th colspan="5">The Present Continuous Tense: Affirmative and Negative Statements</th></tr>
<tr><th>Subject pronoun</th><th>be</th><th>(not)</th><th>verb + -ing</th><th>Contractions with be</th></tr>
<tr><td>I</td><td>am</td><td rowspan="4">(not)</td><td rowspan="4">working.</td><td>I am = I'm; I am not = I'm not</td></tr>
<tr><td>You</td><td>are</td><td>you are = you're; you are not = you're not / you aren't</td></tr>
<tr><td>He / She / It</td><td>is</td><td>she is = she's; she is not = she's not / she isn't</td></tr>
<tr><td>We / They</td><td>are</td><td>we are = we're; we are not = we're not / we aren't</td></tr>
</table>

B Look at picture A below. What are the people doing? On a piece of paper, write five sentences. Use the present continuous tense.

C Work with a partner. Look at pictures A and B. Point to a person and ask a question. Find the differences in the pictures.

What's he doing?

In picture A, he's talking on the phone.

But in picture B, he isn't talking on the phone. He's....

6 COMMUNICATION

A Follow the steps below.

1. Get into groups of four. Read the actions. Look up any words you don't know.

dancing to rap music
exercising at the gym
playing soccer
playing video games
reading a funny book
shopping for a graduation gift
sleeping late
studying for an exam
talking to a boyfriend or girlfriend
texting a friend
waiting for the subway
walking to school
watching a sad TV show
working at an office

2. Write each action above on a piece of paper. Mix up the pieces of paper and place them face down.
3. One student takes a piece of paper but doesn't show the others. The student has one minute to act out the action. What is he or she doing? The other three students have one minute to guess by asking *Yes / No* questions. If they guess correctly, the group gets a point.
4. Take turns as the actor and repeat step 3 until you use all the slips of paper. Which group has the most points?

Are you playing soccer?

Rules

1. You cannot make any sounds when you are acting out the action.
2. You cannot point to other objects as clues. You *can* point to people if they get part of the answer.

B Play the game again. Make slips of paper and use your own ideas.

LESSON B AT SCHOOL

My name is Luis and **I go to** Simon Bolivar University in Caracas, Venezuela. **I'm studying** music with *El Sistema*, a national music program. **I'm taking classes** like math, science, and history, too. Also, this term, **I'm preparing for** the college entrance exam.

1 VOCABULARY

You can also say:
I go to / I'm a student at....
I'm studying / I'm majoring in *IT at the University of Lima.*

A Which subjects and majors from the chart do you know? Tell a partner. Add one more idea. Then tell the class.

B Read about the student above. Answer the questions with a partner.

1. Where is Luis a student?
2. What is he studying?
3. What classes is he taking?
4. What is he preparing for?

C Tell a partner about yourself. Use some or all of the sentences below.

I'm a student at.... / I go to....
I'm majoring in....
I'm taking a... class.
My favorite subjects are....
I'm preparing for the... exam.
I work in....

I'm taking an art class this term.

School subjects and college majors
art
business
engineering
graphic design
history
information technology (IT)
law
math
nursing
science
tourism / hospitality

2 LISTENING

A **Make predictions.** What classes are shown in the photos? Tell a partner.

B **Distinguish speakers.** What class is each man taking? Match each speaker (1, 2, or 3) with a photo. **Track 10**

C **Listen for details.** Read the choices below. Then listen again. Circle the two true answers in each sentence. **Track 10**

	a.	b.	c.
1. He's ______.	a. a good artist	b. majoring in art	c. taking the class for fun
2. He's ______.	a. working in a hotel	b. trying to get a better job	c. taking three classes
3. He's ______.	a. not having fun in class	b. preparing for a class	c. trying to lose weight

D Answer the questions with a partner.

1. Point to a picture above. What class is each man taking? Why is he taking the class? Use your answers in **B** and **C** to explain.
2. Are you (or someone you know) taking any of these classes? Why?

He's taking....

He's trying to....

3 READING

A Look at the photos and captions. Where is Nicolas Ruiz studying this term?

B **Identify main ideas.** Read the interview. Write each question in the correct place to complete it.

Where are you living?
So, are you enjoying Hong Kong?
How's your Chinese?
Which classes are you taking?
So, how's it going?

C **Infer meaning.** Find the words in *italics* below in the reading. Then circle the correct words.

1. A *roommate* is a person you study / live with.
2. If something is *improving*, it is / isn't getting better.
3. *I'm having a great time* means someone is / isn't having fun.

D **Find key details.** Read the interview aloud with a partner. Then answer the questions on a piece of paper.

1. What school is Nicolas studying at this term? Why is he going to this school?
2. Where is he living?
3. What classes is he taking?
4. How is he doing in his language class?
5. Is he enjoying Hong Kong? Why or why not?

E Imagine you can study in another country. What do you want to learn? Make a new interview with a partner.

> So, Kenji, tell our readers about yourself.

> I'm from Tokyo. This term, I'm studying at the Fashion Institute of Technology in New York.

STUDY ABROAD

Track 11

People gather in downtown Hong Kong at night.

In this issue of *Study Abroad* magazine, Emma Moore is talking to Nicolas Ruiz, a student from Argentina. He's studying in Hong Kong this term.

Emma: So, Nicolas, tell our readers a little about yourself.

Nicolas: Well, I'm from Argentina. At home, I'm a student at the University of Buenos Aires. This term, I'm studying at the University of Science and Technology, here in Hong Kong.

Emma: Why this school?

Nicolas: Well, I'm majoring in business, and the University of Science and Technology has a great business school.[1]

Emma: 1. ______________________

Nicolas: Great! The classes are really interesting, and I'm learning a lot. There are also students from all over the world here.

Emma: 2. ______________________

Nicolas: I'm in a dorm[2] with a roommate. He's from Malaysia and he's really nice.

Emma: Glad to hear it. So, tell us about school. 3. ______________________

Nicolas: I'm taking three business classes and one Chinese class.

Emma: 4. ______________________

Nicolas: It's OK. My speaking is improving. Now I can talk to people outside of school.

Emma: Excellent. 5. ______________________

Nicolas: Oh, yeah. I'm having a great time. There's a lot to do and see. It's a really exciting and beautiful city.

Emma: That's wonderful. Thanks a lot for your time, Nicolas, and good luck with your studies!

[1]At a university, there are many *schools* (the school of business, education, law, etc.). Each school focuses on one area of study.

[2]A *dormitory (dorm)* is a school building where students live.

Hong Kong University of Science and Technology

4 GRAMMAR

A photographer

A Turn to page 218. Complete the exercises. Then do **B** and **C** below.

The Present Continuous Tense: Extended Time	
Question	**Response**
What **are** you **doing** these days / nowadays?	I'**m studying** in Hong Kong this term.
Are you **enjoying** Hong Kong?	Yes, I'**m having** a great time!

B Two old friends meet on the street. Complete the conversation with the present continuous tense. Use the words given. Then practice with a partner.

ZACK: Hey, Leo!

LEO: Hi, Zack!

ZACK: How are you doing?

LEO: I'm all right. How about you?

ZACK: Not bad. So, (1. what / you / do) ____________________ these days?

LEO: (2. I / study) ____________________ at State University.

ZACK: Really? (3. What / you / major) ____________________ in?

LEO: Graphic design. What about you? (4. you / work) ____________________ or (5. you / go) ____________________ to school?

ZACK: Both. (6. I / work) ____________________ part-time at a cafe. (7. I / take) ____________________ two classes at City College this term, too.

LEO: (8. What / you / study) ____________________?

ZACK: Photography and art history.

LEO: (9. you / enjoy) ____________________ the classes?

ZACK: Yeah. They're fun and (10. I / learn) ____________________ a lot.

C Make a new conversation. Use your own information in **B**.

5 WRITING

A Complete the interview with your answers.

Studying English: Interview Questions

1. Why are you studying English?

- ☐ I'm doing it for fun.
- ☐ I want to travel.
- ☐ I'm majoring in English.
- ☐ I'm doing it for my job.
- ☐ I'm preparing for an exam.
- ☐ Other: ______________________

2. What are you learning in your English class these days?

____

____

3. How are you doing in your English class? Is your English improving?

____

____

4. Outside of class, how are you practicing English?

____

____

6 COMMUNICATION

A Interview three people. Use questions 1–4 in **Writing A**. Write each person's answers on a piece of paper.

> Why are you studying English?

> I'm preparing for the TOEFL.

> Is your English improving?

> My speaking is, but my listening....

B Work with a new partner. Tell your partner about the three people you interviewed. Use (but don't read) your notes. Which answers are the most popular in your class?

> Juan and Jin Soo are preparing for the TOEFL.

MEMO

NATIONAL GEOGRAPHIC LEARNING

KEIMYUNG UNIVERSITY

MEMO

3 SHOPPING

A luxury shopping mall in Berlin, Germany

Look at the photo. Answer the questions.

1 Is there a shopping mall in your city? What is it called?

2 Do you ever go to these kinds of stores?
- a department store
- a clothing store
- a coffee shop
- a supermarket

3 What are the stores' names? What do you buy there?

UNIT GOALS

1 Identify common foods

2 Talk about things you need

3 Describe your shopping habits

4 Discuss different places to shop and what they sell

LESSON A AT THE MARKET

Farmers' markets are growing around the world. This one is in Otavalo, Ecuador.

1 VIDEO Field of Greens

A Look at the photo. What do you see? Do you have any markets like this in your city?

B Watch the video. What fruits and vegetables do you see? Make a list in your notebook. Compare your list to a partner's.

C Watch the video again. Then answer the questions.

1. What is unusual about the first farm in the video?
2. Do farmers' markets sell foods besides *produce* (fruits and vegetables)?
3. What are the main benefits of shopping at farmers' markets?

D With a partner, plan a dinner menu. Use foods that you can find at a farmers' market. Share your menu with the class. Which pair has the best menu?

2 VOCABULARY

Word Bank
Word partnerships
fresh / frozen / junk **food**

A Practice saying the items in the picture with a partner. Which of these foods do you eat? Tell your partner.

B Work with your partner. On a piece of paper, copy the chart below. Think of examples for each type of food. Use words from the picture and your own ideas.

Fresh foods	Frozen foods	Junk foods	Breakfast foods	Foods you eat every day

C Share your chart with another pair. Then ask and answer these questions.

1. What is one thing in your chart that isn't in the picture above?
2. Which items in your chart do you like? Are there any items you *don't* like to eat or drink?

3 LISTENING

A **Pronunciation: Syllables.** Practice saying the words aloud. Then listen and repeat. **Track 12**

1. fish 2. soda 3. potato

B **Pronunciation: Syllables.** Work with a partner. Read each word aloud. How many syllables does it have: one, two, or three? Guess. Then listen and check your answers. **Track 13**

	1	2	3
1. milk	☐	☐	☐
2. carrots	☐	☐	☐
3. tomato	☐	☐	☐
4. cheese	☐	☐	☐
5. banana	☐	☐	☐
6. cake	☐	☐	☐
7. yogurt	☐	☐	☐
8. apple	☐	☐	☐
9. cereal	☐	☐	☐

C **Use background knowledge.** Look at the two pictures below. What's in each bag? Make two lists. Tell a partner.

D **Listen for gist.** Listen. Which shopping bag is Allison's? Circle it. **Track 14**

E **Listen for details.** Listen. Allison's mom changes one item on the list. Put an *X* on the item in the shopping bag. Write the name of the new item. **Track 15**

F **Listen for details.** How do Allison and her mom talk about the foods they need? Match the items on the left with the words on the right. Then listen and check your answers. **Track 16**

1. I need a ________ of bread.
2. And a ________ of lettuce.
3. A ________ of ice cream.
4. Please get a ________ of carrots, OK?

a. bunch
b. head
c. carton
d. loaf

G Cover your answers in **D–F** and tell a partner: What items does Allison buy for her mom?

4 SPEAKING

A Read the conversation and listen. Underline the foods Ken and Rachel have. Circle the foods they need. **Track 17**

KEN: Rachel, I'm making a shopping list for our barbecue. We have **chicken**. What else do we need?

RACHEL: Let's see... we need some **potatoes**.

KEN: Okay, got it.

RACHEL: We also need **lettuce** and **tomatoes** for the salad.

KEN: And what about drinks?

RACHEL: Let's see... we have **soda**.

KEN: Okay. I'll buy some **juice** then. See you!

B Practice the conversation with a partner. Then make your own conversation. Use your own ideas for the **bold** words.

SPEAKING STRATEGY

C Imagine you are having a class party. Everyone in the class must bring something to the party. Think of an idea and write it on the board.

D Work with a partner. Look at the checklist below. These are things you need for the party. Look at the items on the board. Use the Useful Expressions to talk about the things you have and the things you need for your party.

<u>Class Party Checklist</u>

food

drinks

dessert

napkins, cups, plates

forks, spoons, knives, chopsticks

chairs

E Share your ideas in **D** with another pair.

Useful Expressions
Talking about things you need
Do we need anything?
Yes, we do. We need soda and bottled water.
Let's see... we need...
No, we don't. We (already) have everything.
What else do we need?
We still need...
Nothing. I think we're all set.
Anything else?
Yes, we need...
No, that's it. We have everything.
Speaking tip
You can use *let's see* when you are thinking carefully about something.

5 GRAMMAR

A Turn to page 219. Complete the exercise. Then do **B–F** below.

Count and Noncount Nouns	
Count	**Noncount**
a tomato, an apple	bread, rice
two carrots, three eggs	coffee, sugar

B Study the chart above. With a partner, write *C* or *N* to say if each phrase describes count or noncount nouns.

1. _____ can follow *a* or *an*
2. _____ can follow numbers
3. _____ are always singular
4. _____ have singular and plural forms

C Complete the sentences with *a* or *an*. If no article is needed, leave the space blank.

1. Do you want _____ rice or _____ baked potato with your dinner?
2. Billy wants _____ fruit. Give him _____ apple.
3. Do you usually put _____ sugar in _____ tea?
4. I often eat _____ banana as a snack.
5. Is there _____ salt in this soup?
6. I have _____ cereal and _____ egg every morning for breakfast.

D Read the sentences. Circle *T* for true or *F* for false. Use your own information.

1. I don't like soda because it has too much sugar.	T	F
2. I usually eat pasta once or twice a week.	T	F
3. You can usually find apples, oranges, or some kind of fruit in my refrigerator.	T	F
4. I eat more bread than rice.	T	F
5. I drink at least two glasses of water a day.	T	F
6. I need coffee in the morning to wake up.	T	F
7. I don't eat hot soup in the summer.	T	F
8. I eat too much cake.	T	F

E Which nouns in **D** are count? Which are noncount? Tell a partner.

F Compare your answers in **D** with your partner's.

Soda has too much sugar, but I like it.

Me too. I drink a can of soda every day.

6 COMMUNICATION

A Read about this TV show. Think about what it would be like to live on the island.

There is a new reality show on TV. On this show, people stay on an island in the Pacific Ocean for one month to win money. Here is some information about the island:

- There are a lot of fish in the ocean.
- On the island, there are a lot of coconuts and fruit trees. There's also a lot of sand!
- There's very little water to drink on the island.
- In the afternoon, it is very hot (100 degrees F / 38 degrees C).

B You want to be on the show. For your stay on the island, you can choose six items from the list below. Is there anything you want to add to the list? Write it. Then circle the six items you need.

meat	toothpaste	bananas	bandages	a knife
bottled water	soap	oranges	coffee or tea	matches
rice	sunscreen	magazines	toilet paper	________
bread	a hat	shampoo	vitamins	________

C Join a group of three or four people. Compare your answers. Explain your choices. Together make *one* list of six items.

There's very little water on the island. We need to bring water.

D Explain your final list to the class.

LESSON B LET'S GO SHOPPING!

1 VOCABULARY

A Read the sentences. Review the meaning of the words in **blue** with your instructor. Then complete the sentences so they are true for you.

1. I usually **shop** for things _____.
   a. alone b. with one person c. with a group
2. I **buy** most of my clothes _____.
   a. online b. at stores in **a mall** c. in my neighborhood
3. I _____ buy things **on sale**. The price is lower, so the items are more **affordable**.
   a. often b. sometimes c. never
4. I **spend** _____ **money** on electronics (computers, phones) each year.
   a. a lot of b. some c. no
5. I **pay** for most things with _____.
   a. **cash** b. a **debit card** c. a **credit card**

Word Bank
go shopping = shop (for something)
Opposites
affordable ↔ **expensive**
buy ↔ **sell**
credit or **debit card** ↔ **cash**
on sale ↔ **full price**

B Tell a partner your answers in **A**. Your partner asks you one follow-up question.

I buy most of my clothes at stores in a mall.

What's your favorite store?

2 LISTENING

A Look at the photos above and the list of stores below. Write the correct number (1–4) on each picture. Then write the correct letter (a–d) on each line to match the items with the stores.

Stores

1. a candy store ____
2. an electronics store ____
3. a jewelry store ____
4. a thrift store ____

Items

a. computers, phones
b. used clothes and furniture
c. chocolate
d. rings, necklaces

B **Listen for gist.** Listen. In each conversation, the people are shopping. Where are they? Write *1*, *2*, or *3*. One store is extra. **Track 18**

____ a candy store ____ an electronics store ____ a jewelry store ____ a thrift store

C **Listen for details.** Read the sentences. Then listen again. Circle the correct answer. **Track 18**

Store 1

1. The man is shopping for ____.
   a. candy b. a ring c. a phone
2. The man ____.
   a. goes to another store
   b. spends a lot of money
   c. buys something affordable

Store 2

1. The ____ like(s) the store a lot.
   a. man b. woman c. man and woman
2. The woman says the coat is ____.
   a. expensive b. affordable c. on sale

Store 3

1. The items in this store are ____.
   a. expensive b. affordable c. on sale
2. The man pays with ____.
   a. cash b. a credit card c. a debit card

D Do you ever shop at any of the places in **A**? If yes, what do you buy? Tell a partner.

3 READING

A **Make predictions.** Read the title. Is the article about expensive or affordable stores in Seoul? Tell a partner.

B **Identify main ideas.** Read the article. What does each paragraph (1–4) talk about? Write the words in the reading. One is extra.

Art   Books and Comics   Clothing
Electronics   Food and More

C **Scan for details.** Match the items (1–6) with the place(s) where you can buy them (a–e). Some items may have more than one answer.

1. affordable clothes _____
2. a cell phone _____
3. expensive clothes _____
4. a traditional noodle soup _____
5. souvenirs _____
6. items for the home _____

a. Dongdaemun Market
b. Gangnam
c. Insadong
d. Namdaemun Market
e. Yongsan Market

D **Scan for details.** Write a number or word next to each place. If a number or word is not given, write *NG*.

The number of...

1. department stores in Gangnam: ______
2. malls in Dongdaemun Market: ______
3. stores in Dongdaemun Market: ______
4. stores in Yongsan Market: ______
5. places to eat in Namdaemun Market: ______
6. shops in Insadong: ______

E In your city, what are the best stores or neighborhoods to shop for the things in **B**? With a partner, make a shopping guide for visitors. Share it with the class.

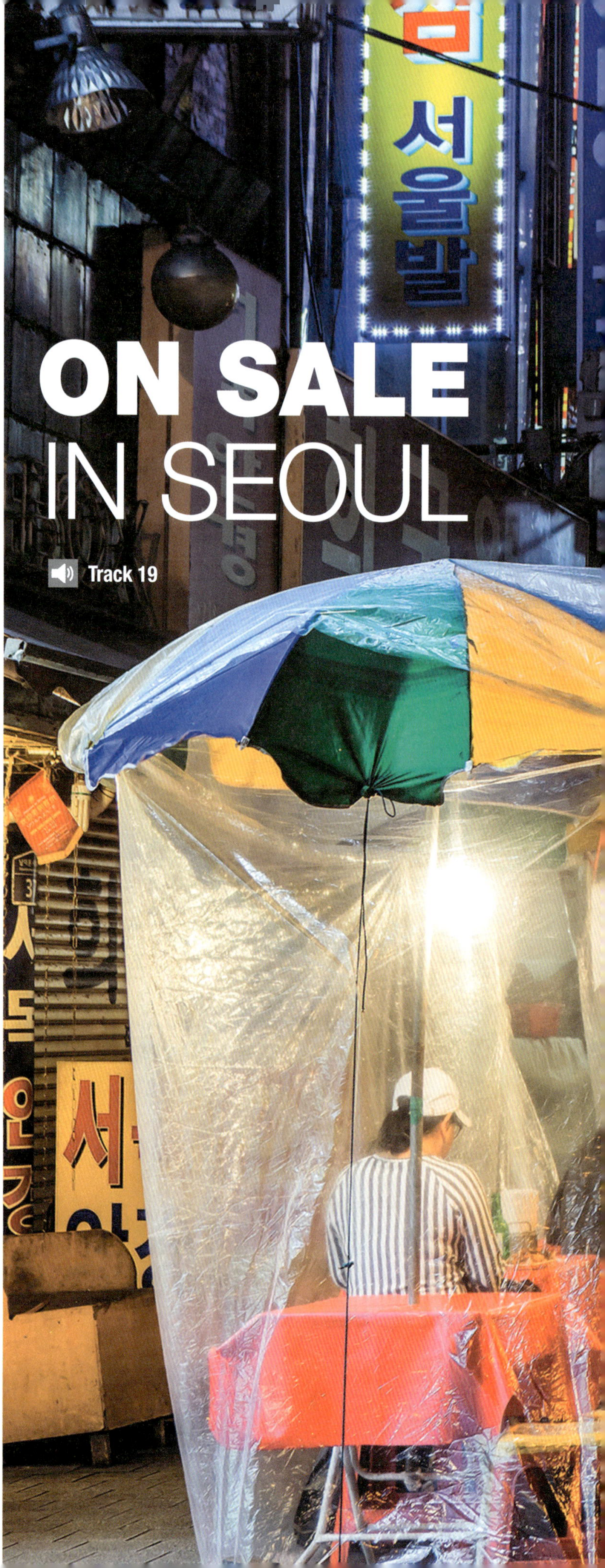

ON SALE IN SEOUL

Track 19

Are you planning to visit Seoul? South Korea's capital city has thousands of stores, so give yourself a day or more to go shopping. Here are some things you can buy:

1. ______________________

Need something to wear? Seoul has a lot of interesting places to shop for clothes. Department stores in the Gangnam neighborhood sell the latest fashions,[1] but they are expensive. For something more affordable, visit Dongdaemun Market. This large shopping area has over 20 malls and more than 25,000 smaller stores. Remember to bring cash and a shopping bag to hold all your items!

2. ______________________

Yongsan Market is the place to go for a new computer, phone, or camera. It has 5,000 stores and many items are on sale.

3. ______________________

Like Dongdaemun, Namdaemun Market is very large and has a lot of shops. These shops sell clothing, items for the home, and many other things—all at affordable prices. Namdaemun is also famous for its food, and there are many places to eat. Most sell traditional Korean dishes, including *kalguksu*—a delicious noodle soup.

4. ______________________

Looking for a souvenir[2] to take home? Visit Insadong, a beautiful, old neighborhood. Many shops sell traditional Korean drawings and other kinds of art. Some items are expensive, but many are affordable.

[1] *The latest fashions* are the most popular clothes of a certain time.
[2] A *souvenir* is something you buy on a trip to remember a place.

Outdoor food stalls like this one are common in Namdaemun.

4 GRAMMAR

A Turn to page 220. Complete the exercises. Then do **B–D** below.

	Quantifiers with Affirmative and Negative Statements	
	Count nouns	**Noncount nouns**
	Do you have **any** friends?	Do you have **any** money?
Affirmative	Yes, I have **a lot of** / **many** friends. Yes, I have **some** friends.	Yes, I have **a lot of** money. Yes, I have **some** money.
Negative	No, I don't have **a lot of** / **many** friends. No, I don't have **any** friends.	No, I don't have **a lot of** / **much** money. No, I don't have **any** money.

B Make the sentences true for you. Circle a verb and then use a quantifier.

1. I buy / don't buy ___a lot of___ clothing online.
2. I have / don't have ______________ expensive shoes.
3. I wear / don't wear ______________ jewelry.
4. I read / don't read ______________ magazines.
5. I drink / don't drink ______________ soda.
6. I spend / don't spend ______________ money on souvenirs when I travel.
7. I have / don't have ______________ video games at home.
8. I buy / don't buy ______________ music online.

C Ask a partner about his or her answers in **B**. Ask a question with *any*. Then ask one follow-up question. Are you and your partner similar or different?

Do you buy any clothing online?

No, I like to try things on.

D Share one way you and your partner are alike and one way you are different with the class.

5 WRITING

A Read the paragraph. Answer the questions with a partner.

1. Where is the writer's favorite place to shop?
2. What kind of store is it?
3. Why is this store her favorite? Give two reasons.

My favorite place to shop is Uniqlo. It is a popular clothing store. I like this store for two reasons. **First**, a lot of their clothes are affordable. In a department store, I can only buy one pair of jeans. At Uniqlo, I can buy two or three. And the store always has things on sale! I'm a student and I don't have much money, so this is important. **Second**, Uniqlo's clothes are casual but nice. Many things are good for school and work. **For these reasons**, Uniqlo is my favorite place to shop.

B Answer the questions in **A** about your favorite place to shop. For each reason you give, explain it with an extra sentence or two. Then use your notes and the example to help you write your own paragraph.

C Exchange your writing with a partner. Read his or her paragraph.

1. Are there any mistakes? If yes, circle them.
2. Answer the questions in **A** about your partner's writing. Do you know this store? Do you like it? Why or why not?
3. Return the paper to your partner. Make corrections to your own paragraph.

6 COMMUNICATION

A Read about Jessie. Then describe her apartment with a partner.

Jessie is a 22-year-old university exchange student. She's living in your country for one year. She lives in a small apartment near her school. This is her apartment.

Jessie doesn't have much furniture.

B Jessie's parents want to visit her. Help Jessie prepare for her parents' visit. Work with a partner.

- What does her apartment have?
- What does her apartment need? Make a list.
- Where can she buy these things? Put your ideas on the list.

Things Jessie needs	Place to shop

She needs some chairs. She can buy them at a department store.

C Compare your list with another pair's list.

MEMO

NATIONAL GEOGRAPHIC LEARNING

KEIMYUNG UNIVERSITY

NATIONAL GEOGRAPHIC LEARNING

MEMO

KEIMYUNG UNIVERSITY

1 STORYBOARD

A Lisa and Eva are roommates. Look at the pictures and work with a partner to complete the conversations. More than one answer is possible for most blanks.

B Practice the conversations with a partner. Then change roles and practice again.

2 SEE IT AND SAY IT

A Describe a person in the picture below to your partner. Don't say the person's name. Your partner guesses the person.

> This person has long hair and...

B Talk about the picture with a partner.

- Where are the people?
- What are they doing?
- Which people are meeting for the first time? How do you know?
- Ask one question about the picture.

C Choose one pair or group of people. With a partner, role-play a conversation of five to six sentences between the people.

> Hi, I'm Felipe.

> Hi, Felipe. Nice to meet you. My name is...

3 TALK ABOUT...

A Get into a group of three people. Follow the steps below.

1. One person chooses a topic from the list and says it to the group.
   - your hobbies
   - why you are learning English
   - your favorite music
   - a country you want to visit
   - your favorite TV show
   - your favorite food
   - your best friend
   - something you don't like
2. Each person in the group asks the first person a question about the topic. That person answers each question.
3. Take turns and repeat steps 1 and 2 for each topic.

> My topic is "your hobbies."

> What do you do for fun?

4 VACATION

Look at the photo. Answer the questions.

1 What is this place like?
2 Do you want to go to this place?
3 What is a popular place for vacation in your country?

UNIT GOALS

1 Talk about weather conditions
2 Give and respond to advice
3 Talk about things you do on vacation
4 Discuss places you want to visit

Climbers relax in hammocks 40 meters off the ground in Monte Piana, Italy.

LESSON A WEATHER

Santa Cruz, Portugal

1 VIDEO Imersão (Immersion)

A Read the list of places below. You are going to see scenes of Portugal. Watch the video and circle the places you see.

a forest	a market	a shopping mall
old buildings	new buildings	a mountain
the ocean	a bus	a soccer field
a movie theater	a beach	a town square

B Would you like to go on vacation in this country? Why or why not? Tell a partner.

C Think about the places in the video. With your partner, write three activities you can do in this country. Which is your favorite? Share your ideas with the class.

2 VOCABULARY

A Work with a partner. Study the information below about the region of Orellana, Ecuador. Then circle the correct words to describe the weather there now.

We often use a form of *be* with these weather words:
The sun is bright.
It's foggy today.

However, you can use *snow* and *rain* as verbs without *be:*
It snows / rains a lot here.
It's raining / snowing now.

1. Right now, it's raining / very windy / cloudy / sunny and it's warm / cold.
2. Today's high / low temperature is 31 degrees Celsius (88 degrees Fahrenheit). That's hot / comfortable / chilly.

B Draw a weather report for your city. Use the example above as a guide. How is the weather in your city the same as or different from Orellana's weather?

Orellana, Ecuador

3 LISTENING

A **Pronunciation: Stress in multi-syllable words.** Practice saying the words aloud. Then listen and repeat. **Track 20**

1. Noun: **rain**
2. Adjective: **rainy**
3. Verb: **raining**

B **Pronunciation: Stress in multi-syllable words.** Read and listen to the sentences. Underline the stressed syllable in each bolded word. **Track 21**

1. It's **chilly** this morning.
2. It's too **windy** for a picnic.
3. What's the **temperature** outside?
4. Are you on **vacation**?

C **Listen for details.** Sam Ford is a weather reporter. He's interviewing Sofia. Where is Sofia, and what is she doing? Listen and circle the correct answers. **Track 22**

1. Sofia is in the city center / the park right now.
2. There are about 2,000 / 20,000 people.
3. Sofia is from Mexico / Brazil.
4. It's 11:45 / 11:55 PM on New Year's Eve.
5. She's running a race of 3.1 / 5 kilometers.

D Listen. How is the weather right now? Circle your answers and write in the temperature. **Track 23**

Current temperature: ___ degrees F / ___ degrees C.

E Discuss the questions with a partner.

1. How's the weather in your city during the winter?
2. Do you ever exercise outside in the winter? How about in the summer? What weather do you like to exercise in?
3. Are there special runs like the one from the audio in your city? When are they?

Would you exercise in this weather?

4 SPEAKING

A Read the conversation and listen. Then complete the conversation with the words in the box. **Track 24**

foggy	pants	shorts
Los Angeles	San Francisco	warm

KYLE: There! All finished!
JULIET: Wait a minute.... You're going to San Francisco, right?
KYLE: Yeah. See? I have T-shirts, ____________, and my sandals.... I'm so excited!
JULIET: But, Kyle, San Francisco is cold and ____________ in the summer.
KYLE: Really? But San Francisco is in California! It's always sunny there!
JULIET: No, it's not. ____________ is ____________ and sunny, but not ____________.
KYLE: Oh...
JULIET: You should take some sweaters and long ____________, too.
KYLE: Oh, OK. Good idea.

B Practice the conversation with a partner.

SPEAKING STRATEGY

C With a partner, choose a situation (1–4) below and create a short role play. Do steps 1 and 2. Then switch roles. Use the Useful Expressions to help you.

1. Your partner wants to drive to a party. It's snowing hard, and the roads aren't safe.
2. Your partner wants to have a picnic on Saturday. The weather forecast is for rain all day.
3. You and your partner are at the beach. It's very hot and sunny. Your partner sunburns easily, and he or she wants to go swimming right away.
4. Your partner wants to go jogging on a cold day. He or she is wearing shorts and a T-shirt.

1. **Student A:** Give advice to your partner in two different ways.
2. **Student B:** Refuse the advice the first time. Then accept it.

Useful Expressions		
Giving advice		
Advice	Accepting	Refusing
(I think) you should take a sweater.	Good idea. OK, I will.	Really? I don't think so. Really? I'd rather not.
I don't think you should drive. You shouldn't drive.	You're probably right.	Really? I think I'll be OK.

It's snowing outside. I don't think you should drive.

Really? I think I'll be OK. I'm a good driver.

But the roads aren't safe.

5 GRAMMAR

A Turn to page 221. Complete the exercises. Then do **B–D** below.

Connecting Ideas with *but, or,* and *so*	
It's freezing in Moscow, **but** it's warm in Rio.	Use *but* to show an opposite idea or contrast.
We can go to the beach, **or** we can visit the zoo.	Use *or* to give choices.
It's raining, **so** we're not having a picnic today.	Use *so* to introduce a result.

B Oona is introducing you to her city. Read the sentences and complete them with *but*, *or*, and *so*.

MY CITY: CHIANG MAI, THAILAND

1. I like to show visitors beautiful places, __________ I take them to Mount Inthanon.
2. During the day, the Old City is famous for its temples, __________ at night it's famous for a large night market.
3. Sometimes it's crowded in the city, __________ I go to Nong Buak Hard Public Park to relax.
4. For a fancy night out, I go for drinks at the Le Meridien Hotel, __________ I have dinner at The Riverside restaurant.
5. City life is expensive, __________ there are plenty of cheap things to do, too. I like to go for a walk in Doi Suthep-Pui National Park.
6. Just outside my city, you can take an elephant __________ boat tour of the jungle.

Doi Suthep, Chiang Mai, Thailand

C Now imagine a visitor is coming to your city. What will you tell him or her? Use the sentences in **B** as a guide. Complete the sentences below with your own ideas. Work with a partner.

1. I like to show visitors beautiful places, ______________________________.
2. During the day, ______________ is famous for ______________, ______ at night ______________________________.
3. Sometimes it's crowded in the city, ______________________________.
4. For a fancy night out, ______________________________.
5. City life is expensive, ______ there are plenty of free things to do, too. I like to ______________________________.
6. Just outside my city, you can ______________________________.

D Share your answers with another pair. Choose the two best tips from both lists and share them with the class.

6 COMMUNICATION

A Interview your partner. Complete the survey with his or her answers. Check (✓) the answers.

Vacation Survey

1. I usually take a vacation in the ______.
   - ☐ spring ☐ fall
   - ☐ summer ☐ winter

2. I like ______ weather.
   - ☐ hot
   - ☐ warm
   - ☐ cold
   - ☐ other (your idea): ______

3. I like to ______ on vacation.
   - ☐ relax
   - ☐ exercise
   - ☐ see things
   - ☐ other: ______

4. What are your favorite activities?

☐ swimming

☐ skiing

☐ surfing

☐ hiking

☐ golfing

☐ mountain biking

☐ other: ______

B Read about the places below and choose one for your partner's vacation.

Cape Town, South Africa

Weather:

- In spring and summer (September–March), it's warm.
- The fall and winter months are chilly, and it rains.

Activities:

This coastal city has beautiful mountains and lovely beaches. They're great for:

- hiking.
- swimming.
- waterskiing.
- surfing.
- relaxing.

Las Vegas, US

Weather:

- Sunny days, comfortable evenings all year.
- In summer, it's 100°F / 38°C.

Activities:

- The casinos, nightlife, and restaurants are popular.
- There are many swimming pools and golf courses.
- Beautiful mountains are just outside of the city for hiking and for skiing and snowboarding in winter.

Sapporo, Japan

Weather:

- There's low humidity all year.
- Winters are cold with a lot of snow.
- July and August are dry and beautiful.

Activities:

- Skiing is popular in winter.
- Summer is great for camping, hiking, and mountain biking.
- The popular Sapporo Snow Festival is held in February.

C Tell your partner your suggestion. Explain your reasons. Does your partner like your suggestion?

1 VOCABULARY

A With a partner, match the vacation activities (a–h) with the photos.

a. ~~pack your suitcase~~	d. go sightseeing	g. post photos online
b. check in to your hotel	e. get a passport	h. unpack
c. buy a plane ticket	f. take photos	

B Answer the questions with your partner.

1. Which activities in **A** do you do before your trip? while on vacation? after your trip?
2. Do you have a passport?
3. On vacation, do you like to go sightseeing? Do you take a lot of photos?
4. Imagine you can go anywhere on vacation. Where do you want to go?
5. Do you ever post photos from your vacations? Do you have any on your phone now? If yes, show one to your partner.

> I don't have a passport. I need to get one.

Word Bank

go on vacation = go on a trip

Opposites

check in to ↔ check out of (a hotel)

pack ↔ unpack

2 LISTENING

A **Infer information.** Look at the photos. What are the people doing? Tell a partner.

B **Listen for gist.** Listen to three conversations. Match each conversation (1, 2, or 3) to a photo. One photo is extra. **Track 25**

C **Listen for context.** Look at your answers (1, 2, 3) in **B**. What are the people doing? Listen. You will hear three possible answers. Circle the correct answer. **Track 26**

1. A B C
2. A B C
3. A B C

D **Make predictions; Listen for details.** Read the three dialogs. Guess the missing words. Then listen again and check your answers. **Track 25**

1. A: ______ I see your passport, please?
   B: ______, here you go.
2. A: ______ you ______ our ______, please?
   B: ______.
3. A: ______ I see a credit card and some form of ______, please?
   B: ______.

3 READING

A **Understand the gist; Make predictions.** Read the title and first paragraph of the article. Answer the questions with a partner.

1. Many travelers have a problem. What is it?
2. Do you ever have this problem?
3. Guess: Think of one tip (helpful idea) the article will talk about.

B **Identify main ideas.** Read the article. Write each tip below in the correct paragraph (1–5) of the reading.

Don't bring books.
Choose simple colors.
Make a list.
Use plastic bags.
Wear your warm clothes on the plane.

C **Scan for details.** Read the questions. Then read the article again and take notes on the answers.

Why should you...

1. make a list before you pack?
2. bring a tablet?
3. buy magazines or books at the airport?
4. pack clothes of certain colors? Which colors are best?
5. wear your warm clothes on the plane?
6. use plastic bags?

D Ask and answer the questions in **C** with a partner.

E In your opinion, which tip is the best? Can you think of any other tips? Tell a partner.

Going on vacation is fun, but packing usually is not. "What should I bring?" travelers often ask. Many people are unsure and pack too much. Then they have to carry a heavy[1] suitcase or pay extra money for it at the airport. How can you pack your things in one easy-to-carry bag? Here are some helpful tips from travel writers Annie Fitzsimmons and Jared Gottlieb:

1. ____________________. When you travel, you only *need* a few things: your passport, credit cards, cell phone, and certain clothes (a suit for work, a sweater for cool weather, shorts for hot weather). What are these things? Make a list. Then pack only the important items.
2. ____________________. Do you plan to read on the trip? Leave books at home. They're heavy. If you want to read, bring your tablet, or buy magazines or books at the airport. When you're done, you can leave them on the plane or at the hotel.
3. ____________________. Bring mostly white, black, gray, tan, and blue clothes and shoes. These colors are easy to mix and match.[2] By doing this, you can pack fewer items.
4. ____________________. Are you going someplace chilly? If yes, wear some of your warm clothes—like sweaters, jackets, or boots—on the plane. These things take up a lot of room in your suitcase and make it heavy.
5. ____________________. Use these bags to organize[3] the items in your suitcase. Put things like your toothbrush, soap, and shampoo in one bag, underwear and socks in another, shirts in another, and so on. By doing this, you use less space in your suitcase. It also makes it easier to unpack!

[1] A *heavy* object weighs a lot.
[2] If you *mix and match* two or more things, you put them together so they look good.
[3] If you *organize* things, you put them together in a neat, orderly way.

Travelers wait for a train in Berlin, Germany

4 GRAMMAR

A Turn to page 222. Complete the exercises. Then do **B** and **C** below.

	Possessive Adjectives	Possessive Pronouns	*belong to*
Whose passport is this?	It's **my** passport. **your** **her** **his** **our** **their**	It's **mine.** **yours.** **hers.** **his.** **ours.** **theirs.**	It **belongs to me.** **you.** **her.** **him.** **us.** **them.**

B Make two wishes about travel—places you want to go or things you want to do. Write each wish on a small piece of paper.

I want to ______________________________.

I want to ______________________________.

Travel wishes

- Get a passport
- Go on a cruise
- Go on a safari in Africa
- Go to another city or country
- Live in another country
- My idea: ______________

C Work in a small group. Follow the steps below.

1. Mix all of the group's wishes together. Put them face down on the desk.
2. One person begins. Take a piece of paper and read it aloud. Then ask: *Whose wish is this?* Try to guess.
3. When you find the person, ask a question about his or her wish.
4. Repeat steps 1–3. Talk about all your wishes.

A: *I want to go to Egypt.* Whose wish is this? Is it yours, Oscar?

B: No, it's not mine. Maybe it's hers—Bianca's.

C: Yes, it belongs to me!

A: Why do you want to go to Egypt?

C: I want to see the pyramids!

5 WRITING

A Read the social media conversation on the next page. Min is posting about her vacation. Answer the questions with a partner.

1. Where is Min going? Where is this place?
2. What happens to Min at the airport?
3. Where is she staying?
4. How's the weather?
5. Lisa gives Min some advice. What does Lisa say?

B On your own, do the following.

1. Think of a place you want to go on vacation. Where is it? Where are you staying? How's the weather there?
2. On the top of a piece of paper, write your name and complete the sentence below.

   I'm checking in at the airport for my trip to ______________!

MIN I'm checking in at the airport for my trip to Palau!
24 hours * Like

YUKI Where is that exactly?
24 hours * Like

MIN It's an island near the Philippines.
24 hours * Like

LISA Have fun! Take lots of photos and make sure to post them!
24 hours * Like

MIN Thanks, Lisa! Oh no! My suitcase is too heavy, so I have to pay extra!
24 hours * Like

LISA I always pack too much, too! ☺
23 hours * Like

YUKI Are you there yet?
3 hours * Like

MIN Yeah. I'm checking in to my hotel. It's near the beach!
3 hours * Like

YUKI How's the weather?
3 hours * Like

MIN It's raining right now, but it's warm. It's beautiful here!
3 hours * Like

LISA You should go swimming with the jellyfish!
3 hours * Like

The jellyfish in Palau can't hurt people.

C Work in a group of three. Sit in a circle. Imagine you are posting online about your trip. Follow the steps below.

1. Give your paper from **B** to the person on your right.
2. Read the sentence on the paper you get. Write a reply below it. Look at the example for ideas.
3. Then repeat steps 1 and 2. Continue for five minutes, "posting" about your vacations.
4. At the end, get your original paper back. Make corrections to your partners' writing. Check for the proper possessive adjectives and pronouns.

6 COMMUNICATION

A Ask a new partner the questions below about his or her vacation from Writing.

1. Where are you going?
2. Where are you staying?
3. How's the weather?
4. What do you like most about the place?

B Repeat **A** with two new partners. Whose vacation is the most interesting? Why?

MEMO

NATIONAL GEOGRAPHIC LEARNING

KEIMYUNG UNIVERSITY

MEMO

5 FOOD

Look at the photo. Answer the questions.

1. Do you know any of these foods? What are they?
2. Which ones do you eat?
3. Do you like them?

UNIT GOALS

1. Order food from a menu
2. Talk about foods you like, dislike, and eat often
3. Talk about healthy eating habits
4. Describe your favorite food

A spread of food and spices

LESSON A WHAT'S ON THE MENU?

Fruit at the Oxford Covered Market

1 VIDEO At the Covered Market

A Watch the video with the sound off. What foods do you see? Tell a partner.

B Watch the video. Write the food each person doesn't like.

meat	fish	tomatoes

1. Jan ____________
2. Richard ____________
3. Amy ____________

C Do you want to go to Oxford Covered Market? Why or why not? Is there a market like Oxford Covered Market where you live? Tell a partner.

2 VOCABULARY

A With a partner, think of a few fruits and vegetables in English. Do you like to eat any of these items? Share your ideas with the class.

B Look at the pictures and the list of drinks. Ask and answer the questions with a partner.

1. Do you ever eat or drink any of these items?
2. Which ones do you like?
3. What other foods and drinks do you like?

steak and baked potato

spinach salad with tomatoes and onions

cheese and fruit

spaghetti and tomato sauce

vegetable soup and bread

rice and beans

fried chicken

tuna sandwich

Common drinks

- coffee
- milk
- orange juice
- soda
- tea

3 LISTENING

A What restaurants do you like? What do you order there? Tell a partner.

B **Listen for details.** Mia and Leo are at a restaurant for lunch. Listen. Circle the items that they order from the bills to the right. Then answer the questions. **Track 28**

1. Which person eats in the restaurant ("for here")?

   ____

2. Which person eats out of the restaurant ("to go")?

   ____

C **Pronunciation: *And, or*.** Listen and complete each conversation with the word *and* or *or.* Notice how *and* and *or* are pronounced. Then practice the conversations with a partner. **Track 29**

1. A: Umm… I'd like the spaghetti with tomato sauce.
   B: OK, that comes with soup _______ salad.
2. A: I'd like a chicken sandwich.
   B: OK, that comes with French fries _______ mixed vegetables.
3. A: What juices do you have?
   B: Apple _______ orange.
4. A: Is that for here _______ to go?
   B: For here.

D With a partner, order your lunch from the items in **B**. Use the words for ordering food and talking about meals to help you.

Word Bank

Ordering food

What can I get you? / Would you like anything to drink?

I'd like a soup and salad, please. / Orange juice, please.

Talking about meals

breakfast (morning), *lunch* (afternoon), *dinner* (evening)

I have eggs and coffee for breakfast.

Date	Server	For here / To go	Order No
			0142

NO		AMOUNT
	MAIN DISHES	
	Chicken sandwich	
	Rice and beans	
	Spaghetti	
	Veggie burger	
	SIDE DISHES	
	Soup	
	Salad	
	French fries	
	Mixed vegetables	
	DRINKS	
	Soda	
	Coffee	
	Bottled water	
	Apple juice	
	Orange juice	
	TAX	

Mia's order

Date	Server	For here / To go	Order No
			0143

NO		AMOUNT
	MAIN DISHES	
	Chicken sandwich	
	Rice and beans	
	Spaghetti	
	Veggie burger	
	SIDE DISHES	
	Soup	
	Salad	
	French fries	
	Mixed vegetables	
	DRINKS	
	Soda	
	Coffee	
	Bottled water	
	Apple juice	
	Orange juice	
	TAX	

Leo's order

4 SPEAKING

A Listen to the conversation and practice it with a partner. Then answer the questions. **Track 30**

1. What can you eat at Tapeo 39?
2. What is perfect for summer? Why?

JASON: I'm hungry.
MARIA: Me, too. Do you like Indian food?
JASON: No, not really.
MARIA: How about Spanish food? I know a fun place.
JASON: Yeah? What is it?
MARIA: It's called Tapeo 39, and they have great gazpacho there.
JASON: What's gazpacho?
MARIA: It's a delicious kind of soup. I like it a lot.
JASON: It's too hot for soup, Maria!
MARIA: Don't worry. It's a cold soup. It's perfect for summer.
JASON: What's in it?
MARIA: Tomatoes, cucumbers, onions, and pepper.
JASON: Sounds good.
MARIA: It is. Oh, and they also have tasty sandwiches.
JASON: Let's go!

Gazpacho

SPEAKING STRATEGY

B Think of two restaurants. Write the information.

Restaurant name: ______________ Restaurant name: ______________
Kind of food: ______________ Kind of food: ______________
Food on the menu: ______________ Food on the menu: ______________

C Make new conversations with your partner. Use the conversation in **A** and your information from **B**, as well as the Useful Expressions, to help you.

Useful Expressions	
Talking about likes and dislikes	
Do you like Indian food? Do you like fish?	Yes! I love it! Yes, I like it a lot. Yeah, it's OK. No, not really. No, I can't stand it.

Hey, Pablo, I'm hungry.

I'm hungry, too. I know a great place for dinner. Do you like Chinese food?

5 GRAMMAR

A Turn to page 223. Complete the exercises. Then do **B** and **C** below.

Simple Present Affirmative Statements		
Subject pronoun	**Verb**	
I / You / We / They	eat	meat.
He / She / It	eats	

Simple Present Negative Statements			
Subject pronoun	***do* + *not***	**Verb**	
I / You / We / They	don't	eat	meat.
He / She / It	doesn't		

B Use the verbs in the box to complete the facts about Sylvie. You will use some words more than once. Check your answers with a partner.

do	drink	eat	go	know	study

Sylvie	You
For breakfast, she...	For breakfast, I...
1. ________ a glass of orange juice. But she (not) ________ coffee. She can't stand it.	1. ____________________
2. ________ eggs and toast. They're her favorite.	2. (not) ____________________ ____________________
After school, she sometimes...	After school, I sometimes...
3. ________ to a cafe and ________ her homework.	3. ________ and ________ my homework.
4. ________ with friends in the library. Then they ________ dinner together.	4. ________ with friends. Then we ________ together.
Italian food is her favorite. She...	________ food is my favorite. I...
5. ________ a good place for pizza and pasta.	5. ________ a good place for ________.
6. (not) ________ there often. It's expensive.	6. (not) ________ there often.

C Now complete the information above about yourself. Tell a partner.

6 COMMUNICATION

A You are having a dinner party. Read about your six dinner guests.

She's from London, England. She plays guitar in a band. She doesn't eat meat. She is Danny's girlfriend.

She's from Manila, in the Philippines. She's an actress. She speaks English, Spanish, and Tagalog. She doesn't drink alcohol.

She's from São Paulo, Brazil. She studies art at the University of London. She likes soccer.

He's from the Dominican Republic. He speaks English and Spanish. He loves spicy food. He plays baseball.

He's from Los Angeles, in the United States. He's an actor. His brother works in South America. He loves Italian food.

He's from Buenos Aires, Argentina. He lives in Canada now. He teaches music at the University of Toronto.

B Plan the party!

1. With a partner, make a menu for the dinner party.

   Think about your dinner guests' likes and dislikes.

2. Choose a seat at the table for each person. Include yourself and your partner.

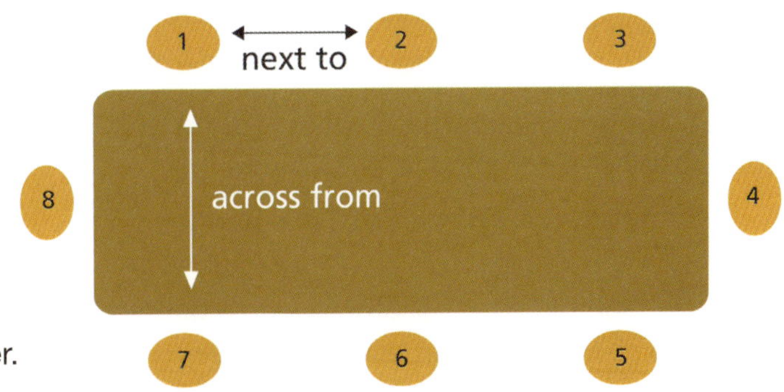

C Get together with a new pair. Explain your menu and table seating.

Here's our menu. For dinner, we are having....

Paula is in seat one. She's next to Tomas. They both like sports. She's across from....

LESSON B EATING RIGHT

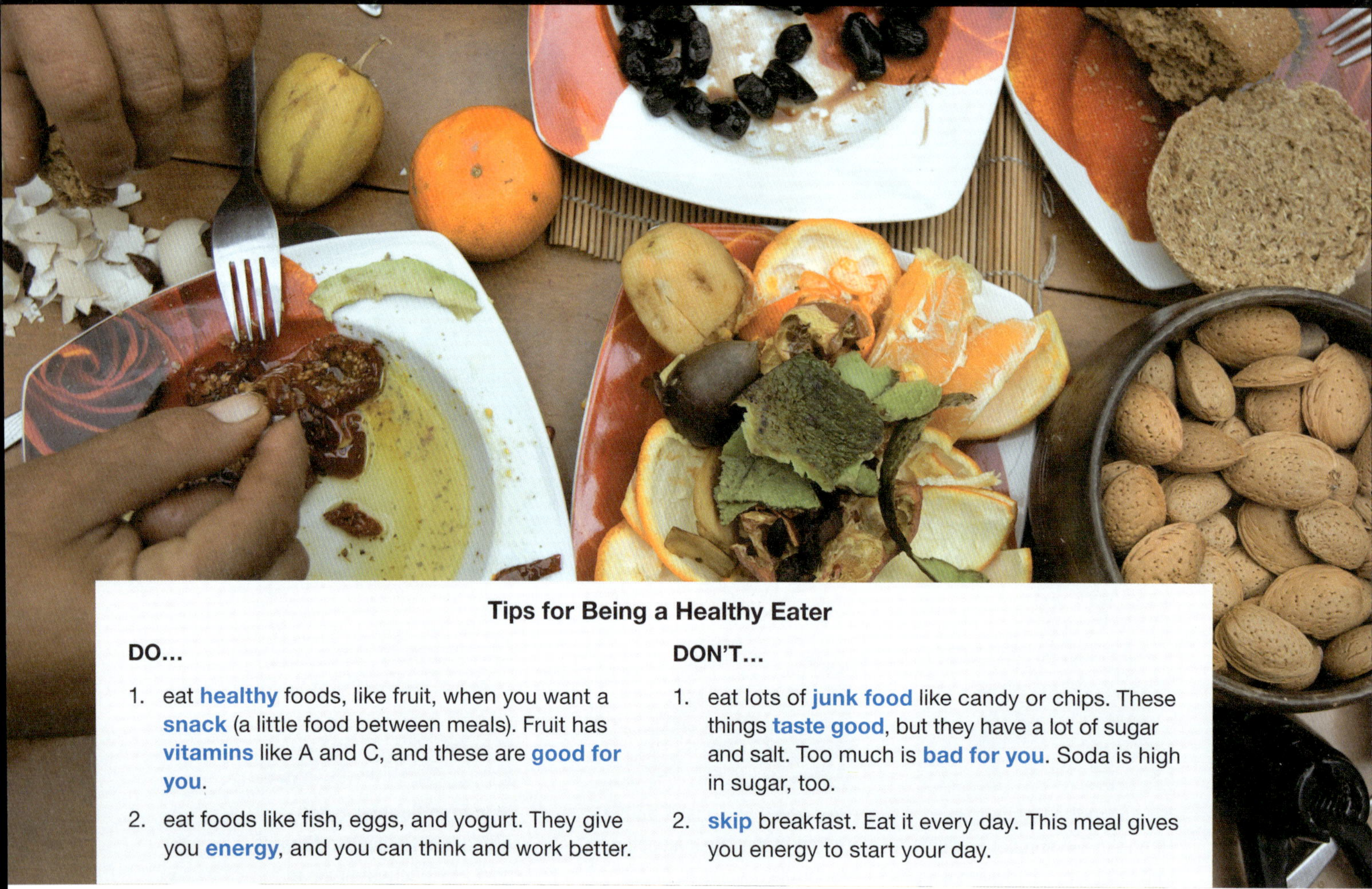

Tips for Being a Healthy Eater

DO...

1. eat **healthy** foods, like fruit, when you want a **snack** (a little food between meals). Fruit has **vitamins** like A and C, and these are **good for you**.
2. eat foods like fish, eggs, and yogurt. They give you **energy**, and you can think and work better.

DON'T...

1. eat lots of **junk food** like candy or chips. These things **taste good**, but they have a lot of sugar and salt. Too much is **bad for you**. Soda is high in sugar, too.
2. **skip** breakfast. Eat it every day. This meal gives you energy to start your day.

1 VOCABULARY

Word Bank

Opposites

good for you ↔ bad for you

healthy ↔ unhealthy

have / eat breakfast ↔ skip breakfast

taste good ↔ taste bad

A Read the tips above. Then answer the questions.

1. To be a healthy eater, what is good to do? What's not good to do? Why?
2. Which tips do you do? Tell a partner.

I don't eat junk food. I don't like it.

B Complete the sentences with a partner. Use new ideas. Then tell another pair.

To be healthy:

1. eat foods high / low in....
2. don't eat.... It tastes good, but it's bad for you.
3. only drink a little.... Too much is bad for you.
4. don't skip....
5. eat.... It gives you energy.
6. eat...for a snack.

C Make a poster with a partner using your ideas from **B**. Share your poster with the class and vote for a winner.

2 LISTENING

A **Make and check predictions.** The items in the photos are used to make a smoothie. Guess: What is a smoothie? Circle your answer. Then listen to check your answer. **Track 31**

a. a soup b. a drink c. a main dish d. a dessert

milk

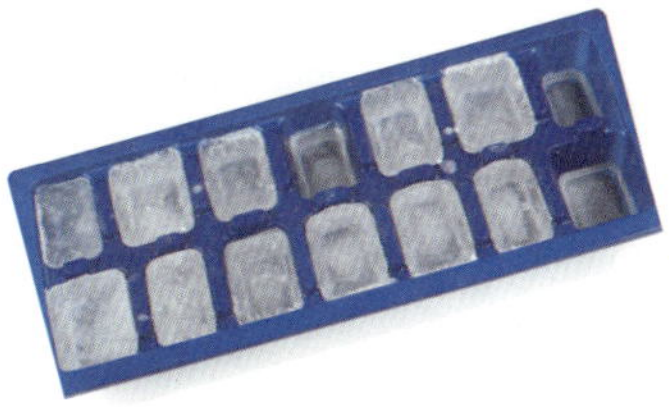
ice

bananas

honey

ice cream

strawberries

oranges

yogurt

B **Listen for details.** Listen again. What is <u>not</u> used to make the smoothie? Put an X on it. **Track 31**

C **Listen for sequence.** How do you make the smoothie? Put the pictures in order from 1 to 7. Then listen and check your answers. **Track 32**

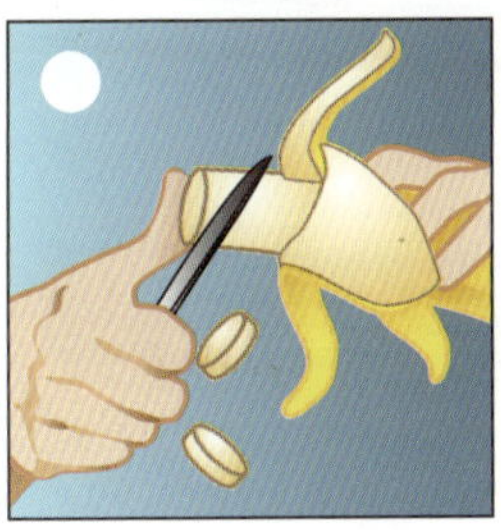
cut it into pieces

blend everything

peel the fruit

add the other ingredients

put oranges in the blender

put ice in the blender

add the other fruit

D Tell a partner how to make a smoothie. Use your answers in **C**.

To make a smoothie, first you.... Then you....

E Do you ever drink smoothies? Are they healthy? What's in them? Tell a partner.

3 READING

A Find the words in *italics* below in your dictionary. Then answer the questions with a partner.

1. Which *illness*—*cancer* or a *cold*—is very bad?
2. Where is your *stomach*? Where is your *skin*? Point to each one.

B **Scan for information.** Read and answer questions 1–3 about your food only.

Student A: Read about chili peppers.

Student B: Read about licorice.

1. Where does the food come from?
2. How do people use it today?
3. Why is it good for us?

C Ask your partner the questions in **B** about his or her food. What are the answers? Take notes.

D **Read for details.** Are statements 1–9 about chilies (C), licorice (L), or both (B)? Write the correct letter.

_____ 1. is / are high in vitamin C

_____ 2. is / are in cold medicine

_____ 3. give(s) you energy

_____ 4. come(s) from Asia and Europe

_____ 5. can help people with cancer

_____ 6. is / are in sweet foods and drinks

_____ 7. make(s) you less hungry

_____ 8. come(s) from the Americas

_____ 9. can stop stomach and skin problems

E Name another healthy food. Answer the questions in **B** about it. Tell a partner.

TWO POWERFUL HEALTH FOODS

Track 33

Chili peppers are a type of fruit from the Americas. They were first used 6,000 years ago! Today, people all over the world, from Mexico to Thailand, use chilies in their cooking.

Chili peppers taste good, but they're also good for us. They are high in[1] vitamin C. This keeps you healthy. Many chilies are also spicy. This spice gives you energy. It also makes you less hungry, so you eat less. Doctors think chili peppers can stop some kinds of cancer, too.

[1] If something is *high in* vitamin C, it has a lot of vitamin C.

Licorice, a type of plant, comes from southern Europe and Asia. Today, when people hear the word *licorice*, they think of candy. In fact, licorice is in some sweet foods (like candy) and drinks (like soda), but it is also a very old medicine.[2] Two thousand years ago, people used licorice for colds and other illnesses. Today, it is still in some cold medicines. People also use it for stomach and skin problems. And now doctors think licorice—like chili peppers—can help people with cancer!

[2] *Medicine* is something you drink or eat to stop an illness.

Red licorice candy has no real licorice in it. Black licorice is much healthier!

4 GRAMMAR

A Turn to page 224. Complete the exercises. Then do **B–D** below.

Simple Present *Yes / No* Questions				Short Answers
Do	you they	like	spicy food?	Yes, I do. / No, I don't. Yes, they do. / No, they don't.
Does	he / she			Yes, he / she does. / No, he / she doesn't.

B Read the sentences. Add one more sentence about eating and health.

Find someone who...	Classmate's name
1. has breakfast every day.	
2. drinks two glasses of water every day.	
3. eats a lot of junk food.	
4. drinks soda every day.	
5. likes spicy food.	
6. takes vitamins.	
7. eats a healthy snack every day.	
8. ______________________.	

C Use the sentences in **B** to ask your classmates *Yes / No* questions. Find a different person for each answer. Write the person's name. The winner is the person to complete the chart first!

Do you have breakfast every day?

No, I don't. But I drink three sodas every day.

That's a lot!

D Tell a partner about three answers from your chart in **B**.

There are 10 teaspoons (almost 50 grams) of sugar in a can of soda!

5 WRITING

A Answer the questions about your favorite food. Write your ideas in a few words.

1. What is your favorite food?
2. Where is it from?
3. What's in it?
4. When do people eat it (for breakfast, lunch, dinner, or as a snack)?
5. Is it good or bad for you? Why?

B Use your notes in **A** to write a paragraph about your food. Use the example to help you.

My favorite dish is paella. It is from Spain. People eat it for lunch. It has rice, chicken, seafood, onions, tomatoes, vegetables, and a spice called saffron. It's delicious and very healthy. It's high in protein, and the vegetables are good for you, too.

6 COMMUNICATION

A Prepare a short talk about your favorite food.

1. Practice: Use your notes from Writing **A** to talk about your food. Do not just read your paragraph.
2. Find a photo, a map, or a video clip to use in your presentation.

B Work in a group of four. Give your presentation. Then listen to the other members of your group. When you listen, take notes. Answer the questions in Writing **A** about your partners' foods.

C Your group talked about four foods. Do you like each one? Why or why not? Take turns asking and telling the group.

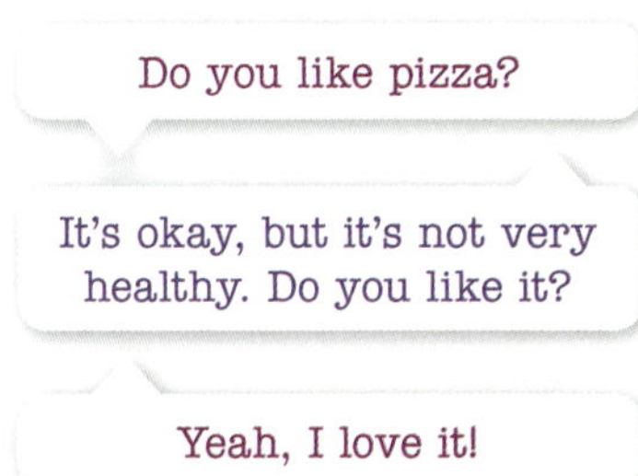

MEMO

NATIONAL GEOGRAPHIC LEARNING

KEIMYUNG UNIVERSITY

NATIONAL GEOGRAPHIC LEARNING

MEMO

KEIMYUNG UNIVERSITY

6 RELATIONSHIPS

Look at the photo. Answer the questions.

1 Are they a big or small family?

2 How many people are there?

3 What are they doing?

UNIT GOALS

1 Identify and ask questions about family members

2 Describe relationships

3 Ask about a person's age

4 Talk about things you have or own

A man plays music for his family in Mongolia.

LESSON A FAMILY

The Cason family standing in front of their house.

1 VIDEO Megafamily

A Look at the picture. What do you think this video is about? Tell a partner.

B Watch the video. Answer the questions. Check your answers with a partner.

1. How many children are in the family? ___________
2. How old is the oldest child? ___________
3. How old is the youngest child? ___________

C Do you have a big or small family? How many brothers and sisters do you have? Tell a partner.

2 VOCABULARY

A Find Amy in the chart below. With a partner, use the list to identify her family members.

Amy's family 25 years ago

1. **grandmother**
2. **grandfather**
3. **mother**
4. **father**
5. **sister**
6. **brother**
7. **aunt**
8. **uncle**
9. **cousin**
10. **grandparents**
11. **parents**

B Cover up the list. Who is each member of Amy's family? Tell a partner.

> Jen is Amy's older sister. Justin is Amy's younger brother.
>
> Susanna is Amy's mother.

C Answer these questions with a partner.

1. Amy lives with her parents and grandparents. Who do you live with?
2. Amy is **close to** her grandmother. She loves her grandmother very much, and they talk often. Who are you close to in your family?

3 LISTENING

A **Make predictions.** Here is Amy's family today. Where are they? Look up the captioned words you don't know.

Hi, it's Amy again. This is my family today.

B **Listen for details.** Now listen and match each name with the correct person above. **Track 34**

a. Amy
b. Tom
c. Sean
d. Gabby
e. Erin
f. Marie
g. Justin

C **Listen for details.** Listen again. Match the questions and answers. **Track 34**

1. Who is a teacher? ___________
2. Who likes school? ___________
3. Who plays sports? ___________
4. Who is Tom's mother? ___________
5. Who is a baby? ___________

Amy
Marie
Gabby
Tom
Erin

D Sean teaches math. His daughter, Erin, likes math at school. Erin is just like her dad. In your family, who are you like? Tell a partner.

I'm just like my mom. We both love art.

Word Bank

*Erin is **just like** her dad.*

*Erin **takes after** her dad.*

4 SPEAKING

A Listen to the conversation between Beth and Lucas. Then answer the questions. **Track 35**

1. How many brothers and sisters does Lucas have?
2. How many brothers and sisters does Beth have?

BETH: You have a really nice family.
LUCAS: Thanks.
BETH: How many brothers and sisters do you have?
LUCAS: I have two sisters and two brothers. I also have lots of cousins!
BETH: Wow, you have a big family!
LUCAS: Yes, I do. What about you, Beth? Do you have any brothers and sisters?
BETH: I have a younger sister.
LUCAS: Are you close?
BETH: Yes, we are. We talk about everything.

Useful Expressions	
Asking and answering questions about family	
How many people are (there) in your family?	(There are) four: me, my brother, and my parents.
Do you have any brothers and sisters?	Yes, I have a sister. / No, I'm an only child.
Are you close (to your sister)?	Yes, I am. / No, not really.

B Practice the conversation in **A** with a partner.

C Use the Useful Expressions to ask three classmates about their families.

Classmate's Name	Family	Brothers and Sisters	Close to...

D Tell a new partner about the people in your chart.

Ruben has a big family. He's close to his sister, Isabel.

5 GRAMMAR

A Turn to page 225. Complete the exercises. Then do **B–F** below.

Possessive Nouns			
Singular nouns	**Plural nouns**	**Irregular plural nouns**	**Proper nouns**
sister → sister**'s**	brothers → brother**s'**	children → children**'s**	Derek → Derek**'s**

B **Pronunciation: Possessive 's.** Listen and repeat. Then practice saying the expressions with a partner. **Track 36**

my sister's son
the boy's name
your mom's friend
his wife's name
Beth's friend
Lucas's family
Mr. Gomez's children

C Look again at the family tree on page 87. Ask and answer the questions below with a partner.

1. How many people are in Amy's family tree?
2. How many people are in her immediate* family?
3. What are her parents' names?
4. What is her brother's name?
5. What is her sister's name?
6. What are her grandparents' names?
7. What is her cousin's name?
8. What is her aunt's name?
9. What is her uncle's name?

*immediate family = parents, children, and close relatives who live in the same home

D Now draw your family tree on a piece of paper. Don't label any of the people.

E Take turns asking a partner about his or her family tree. Use questions like the ones in **C**.

What are your grandparents' names?

F Using the answers in **E**, fill in the family tree with your partner's information.

The British Royal Family *from left* front: Charles and Camilla; back: William, Kate, Harry

6 COMMUNICATION

A Look at this photo of a famous family. What do you know about them? Tell a partner.

B Complete the sentences below about the family in **A**. Check your answers at the bottom of the page.

1. William is Kate's ____________.
2. Kate is William's ____________.
3. William and Harry are ____________.
4. Charles is William and Harry's ____________. William and Harry are his ____________.
5. Camilla is William and Harry's stepmother. Do you know their mother's name? ____________

C Research a famous person's family with a partner. Answer the questions. Find photos of the famous person and his or her family.

1. What is the famous person's name?
2. What is the person's job?
3. Who are four or five people in the person's family? What are their names? How are they related?
4. Are they also famous?
5. What is one interesting thing about this family?

D Get together with another pair.

1. Introduce your person and show a photo. Ask: Do you know anything about this person's family?
2. With your partner, talk about the person's family. Show photos. The other pair will listen and take notes.

This is Angelina Jolie's family. Her husband was Brad Pitt. Angelina and Brad are famous actors.

They have six children. This is her son Maddox. He's from Cambodia. He's adopted.

E What does the other pair remember about your family? Ask them four questions to check.

Who is Angelina's son from Cambodia?

1. husband 2. wife 3. married 4. father, sons 5. Diana

LESSON **B** MARRIAGE

1 VOCABULARY

Kimora's family

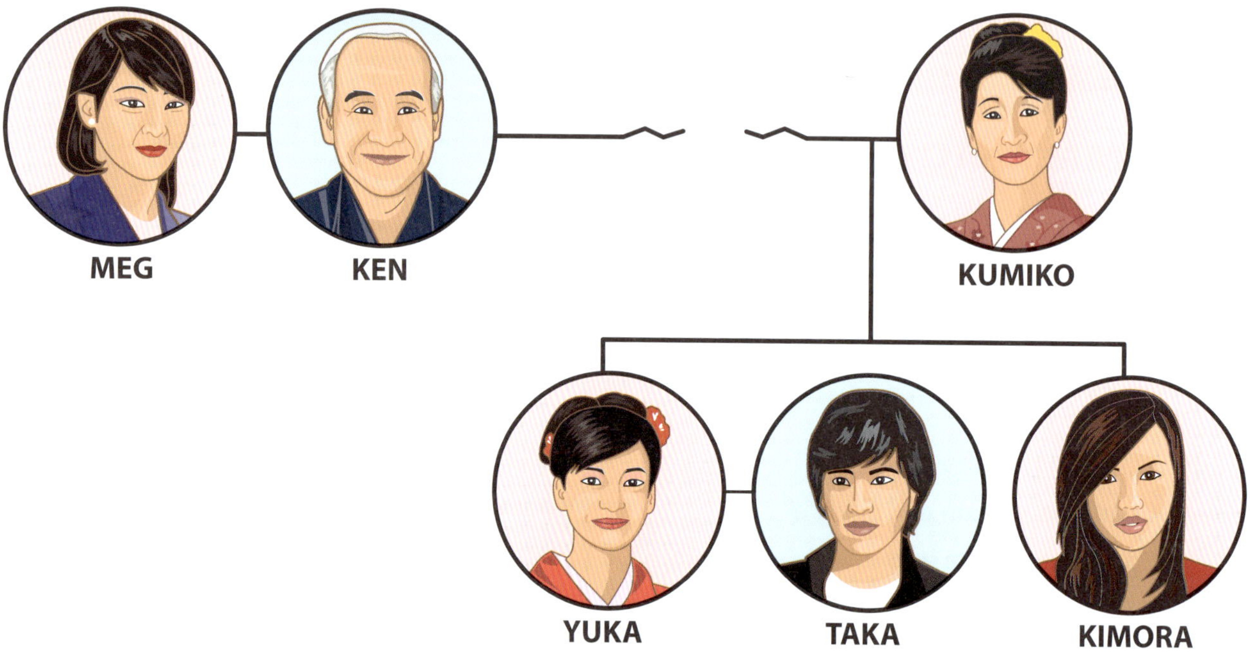

- My parents, Ken and Kumiko, are **divorced**. My dad remarried. His wife's name is Meg.
- My mom isn't married, but she isn't single either. She's **dating someone**. His name is Haru.
- My older sister, Yuka, is **married**. Her husband's name is Taka.
- And me? I'm **single**. I'm really busy with school. I don't have time for a **boyfriend**.

A Work with a partner. Ask and answer the questions about Kimora's family.

Who…

1. is married?
2. is single?
3. is divorced?
4. has a boyfriend?
5. is Kimora's stepmother?
6. is Ken's ex?

Word Bank

Talking about relationships

I'm **dating someone**. My **boyfriend's** / **girlfriend's** name is….

I'm **single**. I'm not dating anyone right now.

She's **married**. Her husband's name is….

He's **divorced**. But he and his **ex**-wife are friends.

B Talk with a partner about three people. They can be family members, friends, or famous people. Are they married, single, divorced, or dating someone?

2 LISTENING

A Think of a famous person. Ask a partner about the person's age.

> How old is Lionel Messi?
>
> He's thirty-three or thirty-four, I think.

How old are you?

I'm… (years old).

16 sixteen
17 seventeen
18 eighteen
19 nineteen
20 twenty
21 twenty-one
22 twenty-two
23 twenty-three
30 thirty
31 thirty-one
32 thirty-two
33 thirty-three

B Look at the chart. What does it show? Tell a partner.

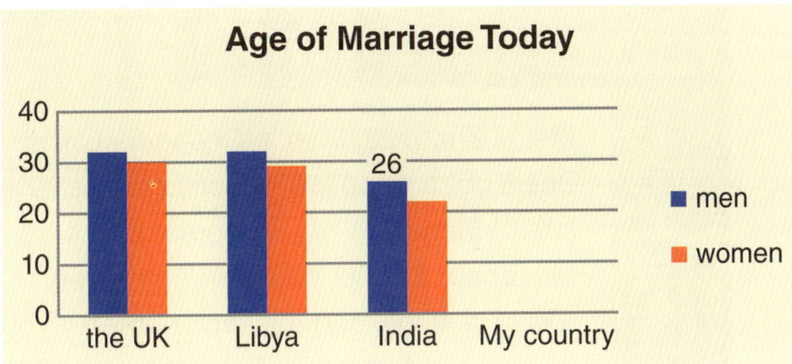

*Lots of people **get married** every year.* (v)

*He's **married**.* (adj)

*They have a happy **marriage**.* (n)

C **Listen for gist.** Listen to the first part of an interview. Complete the sentence with the correct answer. **Track 37**

In some countries, more people are getting married ________ these days.

a. younger   b. later

D **Listen for details.** Listen to the full interview. Write the ages above the bars in **B**. **Track 38**

E Add ages for your country in **B**. Look online. Is your country similar to the other countries? Tell a partner.

A wedding in Mexico

3 READING

A **Make predictions.** Today, many people marry later or not at all. Why? Tell a partner.

B **Read for details.** Read the passage. Then match the statements (a–f) with each person. Two answers are used twice.

Mei Li ______________________

Wei ______________________

a. is dating someone now.
b. has an apartment.
c. 's parents want him or her to marry soon.
d. is single.
e. wants to marry but can't.
f. has a job.

C With a partner, make a short dialog. Use ideas from the reading. Then say your dialog for another pair.

Student A: You're Mei Li's or Wei Yang's parent. You want your child to marry soon. Why?

Student B: You're Mei Li or Wei Yang. You aren't married. Why? Tell your mom or dad.

Mei Li, you're 28. It's time to get married.

Dad, I like my freedom. I've got a good job and....

Yes, but single life isn't easy.

D Answer the questions. Compare your ideas with a partner.

1. Who do you agree with: Mei Li or her parents?
2. In your country, are weddings expensive? Who pays?

TIME TO GET MARRIED?

Track 39

Mei Li Zhao, 28, lives in Chengdu, China. She's got a good job, a nice apartment, and lots of friends. "I've got a great life," says Ms. Zhao. But her parents don't agree. Mei Li is single and they are worried. "You're twenty-eight years old," they say. "It's time to get married."

Mei Li isn't alone. Today in China, more women and men get married in their thirties[1]. But some parents, like Mei Li's, worry about this. In some places in China, it's common[2] for a woman to marry by age 27 or 28. Mei Li understands her parents, but she's not ready for marriage. "Right now," she says, "I like my freedom.[3]"

Wei Yang, 31, lives and works in Beijing. He is also not married. "I've got a girlfriend," he says, "but I can't get married now." Why? In many large cities—like Beijing, Shanghai, and Hong Kong—life is very expensive. A wedding can cost $15,000 or more, and a man's family pays for it. Wei Yang has a job and some money, but not enough for a wedding. "Everyone tells me 'It's time to get married,'" he says, "but today, it's not so easy."

[1]If you are *in your thirties*, you are between the ages of 30–39.
[2]If something is *common*, it is something most people do or think.
[3]If you have a lot of *freedom*, you can do anything you want.

A man and woman in China take wedding photos.

4 GRAMMAR

A Turn to page 226. Complete the exercises. Then do **B–D** below.

Have got			
I'**ve** / You'**ve** / We'**ve** / They'**ve**	**got**	a big family. a nice apartment. a lot of free time. black hair.	**I've got** = I **have got** He'**s got** = He **has got**
He'**s** / She'**s**			

B Circle the things in the box that you have. Then compare answers with a partner.

a boyfriend or girlfriend	a brother or sister	a car	a big family
a phone	a pet	a son or daughter	a job

A: Which things do you have?
B: I've got a younger brother. What about you?
A: I've got a younger brother, too. He's 15. How old is your brother?
B: He's 16.

C Which things do you and your partner both have? Tell another pair.

We've both got younger brothers. Her brother is 15. My brother is 16.

D Which things does everyone in your group have? Tell the class.

We've all got brothers, but they're different ages. Lena's brother is 15. My brother is....

5 WRITING

A Read about Dmitry's family. Then do the following:

1. Find and correct six mistakes with apostrophes.
2. Tell a partner: Who does he live with? Does he have any brothers or sisters? Are they married?

My name is Dmitry, and I'm 21 years old. I live with my parent's in Moscow. I've got an older sister. Shes 29 and married, and shes got a one-year-old daughter. Her babys name is Olga. My sister lives in Kiev with her husband. He's got a big family, and theyre very close. In fact, his mother lives with my sister and her husband. My sister and her husband both work. His mom watches Olga. Its a big help.

B Answer these questions. Take notes.

1. What's your name? How old are you?
2. Who do you live with?
3. Do you have any brothers or sisters? Do you have a favorite aunt, uncle, or cousin?
4. How old are they? Are they married? Do they have children? Where do they live?

Use an apostrophe (') to...
1. join two words (*I have got = I've got, she is = she's*)
2. show possession (*Dmitry's family, my parents' house*)

C Use your notes in **B** to write a paragraph about your family. Use the sample to help you.

D Exchange papers with a partner.

1. Answer questions 1–4 in **B** about your partner.
2. Correct any mistakes.
3. Give the paper back to your partner.
4. Make corrections to your paragraph.

6 COMMUNICATION

A Take the survey. Mark your top three answers.

The perfect mate*: What's important to you?	
He's got... / She's got...	
☐ a college degree.	☐ a handsome / beautiful face.
☐ a lot of money.	☐ a nice personality.
☐ the same interests as me.	☐ my idea: ____________
*Your *mate* is your romantic partner (your husband, wife, boyfriend, or girlfriend).	

B Work in a small group. Tell them your answers. Explain your reasons.

For me, the perfect mate has got....

C Now answer these questions together.

1. Are men's and women's answers similar or different?
2. What answers from **A** are the most common in your group? Tell the class.

MEMO

NATIONAL GEOGRAPHIC LEARNING

KEIMYUNG UNIVERSITY

MEMO

1 SEE IT AND SAY IT

A Look at the photos. Answer the questions about each place with a partner. Complete the sentence.

1. What season does this look like?
2. How's the weather?
3. What's the temperature?
4. In Punta Cana, it's __________________, but in Harbin it's __________________.

B Your partner is going on vacation to one of the places above. What should he or she pack? Use ideas in the box and one of your own. Explain your choices.

a camera	boots
a coat	sandals
a hat	shorts
a swimsuit	sunscreen
an umbrella	my idea: __________

Student A: You're going to Punta Cana.

Student B: You're going to Harbin.

It's very cold there now, so I think you should pack a coat.

Good idea. I will.

2 SEE IT AND SAY IT

A Look at the picture of the food court. Answer the questions.

1. What food and drinks are healthy?
2. What food and drinks are unhealthy?
3. What food and drinks do you like?
4. Look at the people. What are they doing?

B Imagine you are in the food court. Follow the directions.

1. Choose a place and order some food.

   Student A: You are the server. Ask your partner for his or her order.

   Student B: Order something to eat and drink.
2. Change roles and repeat step 1.

C Think of a new restaurant for the food court. Answer the questions.

1. What kind of restaurant is it (Korean, Italian, Mexican, etc.)?
2. What is your new restaurant called? Give it a name.
3. What food and drinks are on the menu? Make a list.

D Share your ideas in **C** with another pair.

3 HE SPEAKS SPANISH

A Look at the picture. What things does this person have in his backpack? Tell a partner.

> He's got a dictionary in his backpack.

B What do you know about this person from the things in his backpack? Make sentences. Use the verbs in parentheses.

1. (be) ______________________________.
2. (speak) ____________________________.
3. (be) ______________________________.
4. (go) ______________________________.
5. (like) _____________________________.
6. (play) _____________________________.
7. (have) _____________________________.
8. (study) ____________________________.

C Take four or five things from your backpack or purse and put them on your desk. Then look at your partner's things. What do you know about your partner from his or her things? Ask your partner questions.

> You have keys. Do you drive?

> No, I don't. These are my house keys.

7 TIME

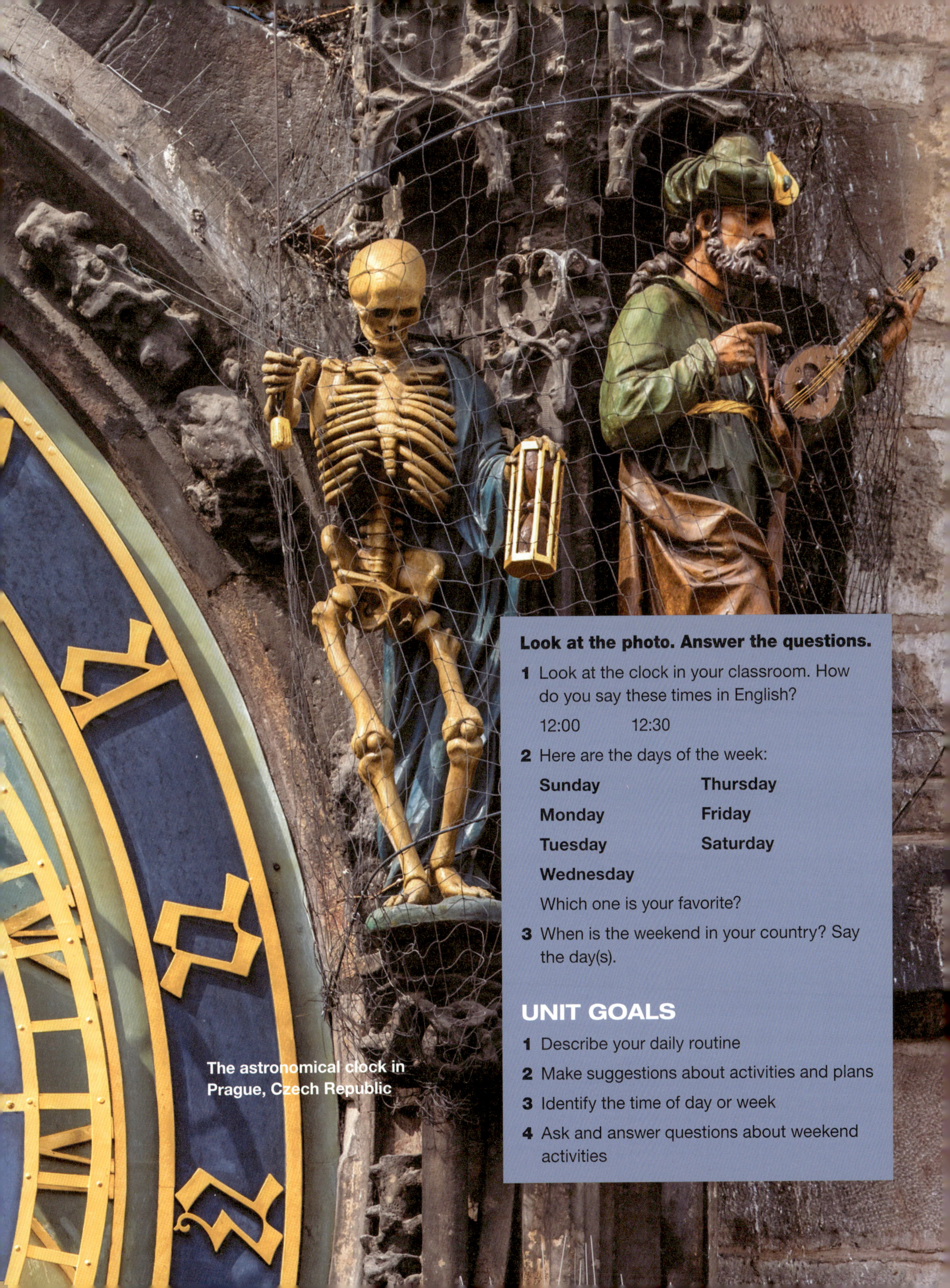

The astronomical clock in Prague, Czech Republic

Look at the photo. Answer the questions.

1. Look at the clock in your classroom. How do you say these times in English?

   12:00 12:30

2. Here are the days of the week:

Sunday	**Thursday**
Monday	**Friday**
Tuesday	**Saturday**
Wednesday	

   Which one is your favorite?

3. When is the weekend in your country? Say the day(s).

UNIT GOALS

1. Describe your daily routine
2. Make suggestions about activities and plans
3. Identify the time of day or week
4. Ask and answer questions about weekend activities

LESSON A MY ROUTINE

People rush through a busy train station in Germany.

1 VIDEO Late for Work

A Before you watch, do this:

1. Look up the word *late* in your dictionary.
2. Look at the pictures and the vocabulary on page 105.

B The man in the video starts work at 9:00. Watch the first 30 seconds. Circle your answer.
The man is / isn't late for work.

C Watch the entire video. What does the man do in the video? Put the events in order from 1 to 7.

____ He washes his face. ____ He reads a text message. ____ He gets dressed.
____ He wakes up. ____ He has breakfast. ____ He leaves home.
____ He brushes his teeth.

D Answer the questions with a partner.

1. Look at the sentence in **B** again. Is the man late for work? How do you know?
2. Does this ever happen to you?

2 VOCABULARY

A Study the times below. Then cover up the words and take turns telling the time with a partner.

What time is it?

It's....

five after four; **four-oh-five**

nine fifteen; **quarter after nine**

eleven forty-five; **quarter to twelve**

two (o'clock)

eight thirty; **half past eight**

two fifty-five; **five to three**

B Practice telling the times shown below with a partner. Then read about Hiro's daily routine.

He **wakes up** at 7:30 and has breakfast.

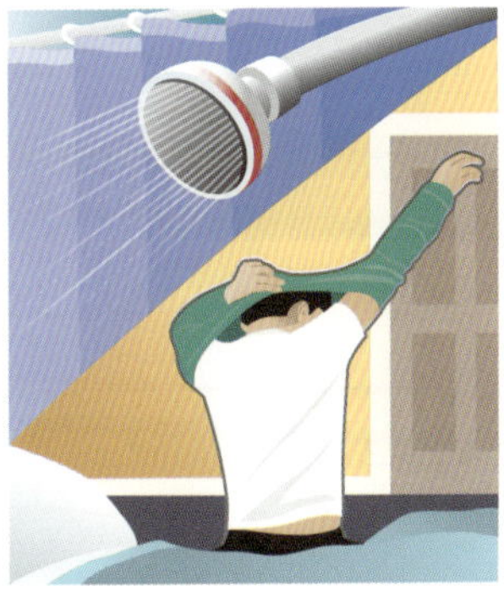

Then he **takes a shower** and **gets dressed**.

He **leaves home** at 8:20 and goes to school.

His classes **start** at 9:00 and **finish** at 4:00.

At 4:50, he studies English.

After that, he **goes home** at 5:45.

He eats dinner at 8:00. He **goes to bed** at midnight.

C Use the words in **B** to tell your partner about your daily routine.

I wake up at 5:30.

That's early!

Word Bank
early = before the usual time

3 LISTENING

A Look at the words *yesterday*, *today*, and *tomorrow* in the box. Then complete the sentences. Compare answers with a partner.

If today is Friday, then tomorrow is ____________. Yesterday was ____________.

Yesterday ←	Today / Tonight	→ Tomorrow
Monday	Tuesday	Wednesday

B **Listen for gist.** Pilar and Alma are talking about Pilar's plans for today and tomorrow. Write *today* or *tomorrow* for each activity. **Track 40**

1. go to school ____________
2. have a piano lesson ____________
3. see a movie ____________
4. study English ____________
5. take a swimming class ____________
6. take a test ____________

C **Listen for details.** Write your *today* answers from **B** on lines 1–4 below. When does Pilar plan to do each of these activities? Listen again and write the start and finish times. **Track 40**

Activity	Start Time	Finish Time
1. ____________	____________	____________
2. ____________	____________	____________
3. ____________	____________	____________
4. ____________	____________	____________

D Tell a partner about Pilar's day. Pilar goes to school at....

E **Pronunciation: Numbers.** Listen and repeat. Notice the different stress. **Track 41**

13 / 30 14 / 40 15 / 50 16 / 60 17 / 70 18 / 80 19 / 90

F **Pronunciation: Numbers.** Listen to the sentences. Circle the correct answer. **Track 42**

1. I wake up at 6:14 / 6:40 every morning.
2. The train to school takes about 19 / 90 minutes.
3. She drives 17 / 70 kilometers to work.
4. After dinner, I study for an hour and 15 / 50 minutes.
5. It's his birthday today. He's 16 / 60 years old.

G **Pronunciation: Numbers.** Listen again and check your answers. Take turns saying the sentences in **F** with a partner. **Track 42**

4 SPEAKING

A Listen to the conversation. Then complete the sentences with a partner. Circle the correct answer. **Track 43**

1. Adriano Jessie Both ...want(s) to eat French food tonight.
2. Adriano Jessie Both ...want(s) to see the new superhero movie.
3. Adriano Jessie Both ...want(s) to see the James Bond movie.

ADRIANO: What do you want to do tonight, Jessie?
JESSIE: I don't know. Hey, let's have dinner at that new French restaurant.
ADRIANO: Hmmm... I don't really like French food. And I'm not very hungry.
JESSIE: OK, well, we could see a movie.
ADRIANO: Yeah, that sounds good. Let's see the new superhero movie.
JESSIE: Hmmm... I don't really want to see that. What else is playing?
ADRIANO: Well, the new James Bond movie is at the AMC Theater.
JESSIE: Great idea. When is it playing?
ADRIANO: At 8:15.
JESSIE: At 8:50?
ADRIANO: No, *8:15*. And there's a late show at midnight.
JESSIE: Midnight is late! Let's go to the 8:15 show.
ADRIANO: OK!

B Practice the conversation with a partner.

SPEAKING STRATEGY

C Use the Useful Expressions to complete the dialogs. Then practice with a partner.

1. A: What do you want for lunch?
   B: ________________ Mexican food.
   A: ________________. I love Mexican food!
2. A: What do you want to do after class?
   B: ________________ play video games.
   A: ________________ video games.
   B: OK, well, ________________ see a movie.
   A: ________________. What do you want to see?

Useful Expressions

Making suggestions

Making a suggestion
Let's see a movie.
We could see a movie.
Saying *yes*
(That) sounds good.
Good / Great idea.
Saying *no* politely
I don't really like French food.
I don't really want to see that movie.

D Add three or four more lines to dialog 2 in **C**.

Student B: Suggest a movie to see.
Student A: You don't want to see Student B's movie. Suggest another idea.
Students A & B: Agree on a movie and a time to see it.

5 GRAMMAR

A Turn to page 227. Complete the exercises. Then do **B–D** below.

Prepositions of Time	
When is your class?	It's **on** Monday(s). / It's **on** Tuesday night.
	It's **in** the morning / afternoon / evening. It's **at** night.
	It's **at** 8:30 / noon.
	It's **from** 4:00 **to** 5:30. / It's **from** Tuesday **to** Saturday.

B Complete the answer choices with *in*, *at*, *on*, *from*, or *to*. Then choose the answers that are true for you.

1. When do you like to study?
   a. _______ the morning
   b. _______ the afternoon
   c. _______ the evening
   d. late _______ night
2. When do you do most of your homework?
   a. _______ weekdays
   b. _______ Saturdays and Sundays
   c. both
3. What day is your birthday this year?
   a. It's _______ Monday.
   b. It's _______ Tuesday.
   c. It's _______ Wednesday.
   d. other: _______________

People study at the library at Colegio de San Nicolas in San Michoacan, Mexico.

4. You can see a movie with your friends _______ noon or _______ midnight.
   Which do you choose? _______________
5. What is your favorite subject at school? What time does the class meet?
   My favorite subject is _______________.
   The class is _____ _______________ (day(s) of the week) from _______ (start time) _____ _______ (end time).

C Now interview a partner. Use the questions in **B**. Take notes.

D What is one new thing you know about your partner now? Tell him or her.

You do your homework on weekdays and Saturdays and Sundays. I think you're a serious student.

Cyclists and joggers, Portland, Oregon, US

6 COMMUNICATION

A Read the directions below.

1. At the top of the schedule, write today's day (Monday, Tuesday, etc.) and the next two days.
2. Complete the calendar with your schedule for these three days (school, work, English or music lessons, an appointment, seeing friends, etc.). You can also add new ideas. Write the activities next to the times in the calendar. If you have no plans, leave the time blank.

9:00 AM			
10:00 AM			
11:00 AM			
NOON			
1:00 PM			
2:00 PM			
3:00 PM			
4:00 PM			
5:00 PM			
6:00 PM			
7:00 PM			

B Work with a partner. Read the example. Then find time in both your schedules to do the three activities together.

- practice English
- see a movie
- your idea: ______________________

A: Let's study together for the test. Are you free today at 1:00?
B: No, sorry, I'm busy. Are you free tomorrow?
A: Well, I have classes from 11:00 to 4:00, but then I'm free.
B: OK, let's meet at 4:15.
A: That sounds good!

LESSON B HAVE A GOOD WEEKEND

People at a party in Amsterdam.

1 VOCABULARY

A Look at the photo. Where are these people? Do you ever do this on the weekend with your friends? Tell a partner.

B Look at the activities with *go* in the Word Bank and read sentences 1–4. Then complete 5–10.

On the weekend, I usually...

1. go for a walk. (a walk)
2. go dancing. (dance)
3. go to a party. (a party)
4. go out with friends. (with friends)
5. ______. (the movies)
6. ______. (a bike ride)
7. ______. (shop)
8. ______. (a friend's house)
9. ______. (with my family)
10. ______. (the gym)

Word Bank

Activities with *go*

go + *-ing* verb
go dancing

go to + a place
go to a party / the beach

go for + an activity
go for a walk

go out + *with* + someone
go out with friends

C In **B**, check (✓) the activities you do on the weekend.

D Compare your answers with a partner's. Are your weekends similar or different? Do you do other activities?

2 LISTENING

A Read the sentences. Then tell a partner: Is a *day off* a free day or a workday?

Tomorrow is my day off. I don't work or go to school.

B **Listen for details.** Nick and Kelly are talking. Listen. Check (✓) the days Nick works. Put an *X* on his day(s) off. **Track 44**

☐ Monday

☐ Friday

☐ Saturday

☐ Sunday

C **Listen for details.** What is good and bad about Nick's day(s) off? Listen. Write one word in each blank. **Track 45**

Good: Most people are at work or ______________. Most places aren't ______________.

Bad: Nick's friends are ______________. He does most things ______________.

D **Listen for details.** Listen again. Check (✓) the things Nick does on his day off. **Track 45**

☐ He goes shopping.

☐ He goes to the movies.

☐ He does homework.

☐ He goes for a bike ride.

☐ He wakes up late.

☐ He goes out with friends.

E Is your day off similar to or different from Nick's? Why? Tell a partner.

3 READING

A Look at the pictures in the reading. What are the people doing? Tell a partner.

B **Make predictions.** Match a person (1, 2, 3, or 4) with one or more activities (a–f) below.

Person

1. The Couch Potato ___________
2. The Workaholic ___________
3. The Party Animal ___________
4. The Health Nut ___________

Activity

a. likes to exercise
b. wakes up late on the weekend
c. goes out all night
d. doesn't like to go out on weekends
e. is always thinking about work or school
f. wakes up early

C **Check predictions; Read for specific information.** Now read the article. Check your answers in **B**.

D Work in a group of 3–4 people. Answer the questions.

1. What kind of weekend person are you? Why? Which type is most common in your group?
2. Think of something you want to do this weekend. Suggest it to your partners. Can you all agree?
3. What kind of weekend person is your best friend?

THE HEALTH NUT

For you, the weekend isn't a time to relax; you want to go out and do things! You usually wake up early (yes, even on the weekend) and go for a walk, a run, or a bike ride. All week, you're inside at school or work. On the weekend, it's time to go outside and be active!

WHAT KIND OF WEEKEND PERSON ARE YOU?

Track 46

For many people, the weekend is a time to relax and have fun. But not everyone has fun in the same way. Here's how different people spend their weekends. What type of person are you?

THE COUCH POTATO

What's your perfect weekend? Sleeping late, watching TV, and playing video games. Sure, you like to spend time with[1] friends—but only at home.

[1] If you *spend time with* people, you do something together.

THE WORKAHOLIC

It's the weekend and it's time to relax... but not for you. The Workaholic is always busy: working, studying, talking on the phone, texting classmates, or checking emails. When you go out with friends on the weekend, you're thinking about your homework or your next exam.

THE PARTY ANIMAL

For you, the weekend is all about fun—and lots of it. Your night starts at 9:00 or 10:00. You go dancing or to a party with friends. Later, you go home and sleep all day. Then you wake up in the afternoon and do it all again!

4 GRAMMAR

A Turn to page 228. Complete the exercises. Then do **B** and **C** below.

Simple Present *Wh-* Questions				
Question word	***do / does***	**Subject**	**Verb**	**Answers**
Who	do	you	study with?	(I study with) Maria.
What	does	she	do on Saturdays?	(She) goes out with friends.
When	do	they	have class?	(They have class) at 9:00.
		we		(We have class) on Mondays.
Where	does	he		(He has class) in Room 3B.

B Read about Zoe's weekend. Unscramble questions 1–4. Start each sentence with a question word. Then ask and answer the questions with a partner.

On Saturday, Zoe...	On Sunday, Zoe...
• works at a department store from 9:00 AM to 3:30 PM. • goes to the gym in the afternoon. • goes out with friends at night.	• wakes up at 11:00 AM. • goes for a bike ride in the afternoon. • studies in the evening.

1. Zoe / what / do / on Saturday afternoon / does
   ________________? She goes to the gym________________.
2. she / work / does / when
   ________________? ________________.
3. does / work / she / where
   ________________? ________________.
4. who / on Saturday night / Zoe / does / go out with
   ________________? ________________.

C Write four more questions about Zoe's schedule. Use different question words. Then ask and answer the questions with a partner.

1. ________________
2. ________________
3. ________________
4. ________________

What time does Zoe get up on Sunday?

5 WRITING

A Read the texts between Raquel and her friends, Monika and Alex. Answer the questions with a partner.

1. What does Raquel suggest?
2. Who says *yes*? What does the person suggest?
3. What do these symbols mean in the texts?

B Write a text to a partner. Suggest something to do tonight or this weekend. Say when and where it is.

C Exchange texts with your partner. Read his or her message. Then write a text back saying *yes* or *no*. If you say *no*, give a reason.

D Repeat **B** and **C** with a new partner.

6 COMMUNICATION

A Read the questions on the left side of the chart. In the *Me* column, check (✓) the activities you do.

Do you...	Me	Classmates	Question	Details
watch TV?			What... ?	
go shopping?			Where... ?	
wake up late?			When... ?	
go out with friends?			Where... ?	
do homework?			What... ?	
spend time with family?			Who... ?	
your idea: ______________			______________	

B Interview your classmates. For each question, find a different person to answer *yes*. Write the classmate's name. Ask another question to get more details.

Do you watch TV on the weekend?

Yes, I do.

What do you watch?

On Sunday night, I watch....

C Read your notes. What is the most interesting answer? Tell the class.

MEMO

NATIONAL GEOGRAPHIC LEARNING

MEMO

KEIMYUNG UNIVERSITY

8 CITY LIFE

Traffic speeds by on a busy night in Shanghai, China.

Look at the photo. Answer the questions.

1. What city is this? Do you know anything about this city?
2. Is your city a good place to live? Why or why not?
3. What do you like most about your city? What do you dislike?

UNIT GOALS

1. Identify places in a neighborhood
2. Ask for and give directions
3. Give your location
4. Explain why a city is or isn't a good place to live

LESSON A MY NEIGHBORHOOD

The Stockholm Metro is famous for its art.

1 VIDEO My City: Stockholm

Word Bank

diverse = different

exhibition = a public art event

A Read the list below. Then watch the video with the sound off. Check (✓) the things Stockholm has.

Stockholm has ______________.

- ☐ beautiful old buildings
- ☐ a river
- ☐ nice parks with trees and flowers
- ☐ a lot of very large cars
- ☐ many immigrants (people from other countries)
- ☐ some noise from nearby factories
- ☐ a beautiful subway
- ☐ many well-dressed people

B Watch the video. Match the phrases to form sentences from the video. One phrase is extra.

1. Stockholm is known for its long summer days _____
2. The people here are as diverse _____
3. It's part of the lifestyle to _____
4. The Stockholm Metro has the world's longest art exhibition. _____

a. look good and dress nice.
b. and the never-ending, icy winter nights.
c. It's 110 kilometers.
d. as the fruits and flowers on sale.
e. stay up late at night.

C Answer the questions with a partner.

1. What is something you learned about Stockholm? Do you want to visit this city?
2. Does your city have any of the things in **A**?
3. My city is known for ____.

2 VOCABULARY

A Look at this list of places found in a **neighborhood** (the area around your home). Which words do you know? Do you know any other words that end in *club*, *salon*, *shop*, *stand*, *station*, or *store*?

health club	**coffee shop**	**train station**
hair salon	**newsstand**	**grocery store**

Word Bank

health club = **gym**
coffee shop = **cafe**
newsstand = **kiosk**
grocery store = **supermarket**
ATM = **cash machine**

B Complete the location names below by using the words in the box. Then look at the photos and label the places. Compare your answers with a partner's.

____

____

____

____

____

____

____

____

____

____

1. ATM
2. book ________
3. bus ________
4. copy ________
5. department ________
6. gas ________
7. nail ________
8. night ________
9. police ________
10. taxi ________

club	station
stand	shop
salon	store

C What do you do at the places in **A** and **B**? Which places do you visit often? Discuss with a partner.

I go to the train station every morning. I take the train to school.

The train station in Lubeck, Germany

3 LISTENING

A **Pronunciation: Stress in compound noun phrases.** Listen and repeat. What do you notice about the stress pattern of these nouns? **Track 47**

1. health club
2. coffee shop
3. train station
4. taxi stand
5. copy shop
6. nail salon

B **Listen for details.** Read the sentences. Then listen to Pablo and Yuki's conversation. Circle T for *true* or F for *false*. **Track 48**

1. It's Pablo's neighborhood.	T	F
2. Yuki lives nearby.	T	F
3. Yuki has a lot of homework.	T	F
4. The library opens at noon.	T	F
5. Yuki wants to buy a book.	T	F
6. The bookstore has a cafe.	T	F

C **Make and check predictions.** Look at the chart. Can you guess the answers? Listen again and complete the chart with other ways of saying these ideas. **Track 48**

Original idea	What you hear
1. How are you?	______ going?
2. Is this your neighborhood?	______ you ______ around here?
3. Where are you going?	Where are you ______?
4. drink a cup of coffee	______ a cup of coffee
5. Don't talk (to me).	No ______ allowed.

D Where is the most popular place to hang out in your neighborhood? Describe it to a partner.

WORLD LINK

Do you live near a train line or bus route? When does the first and last train or bus run? How many stations or stops are there? Share your information with your class.

4 SPEAKING

A Min Chul and Jan are driving to the movies. Look at the map and listen to their conversation. What are they looking for? Where is it? **Track 49**

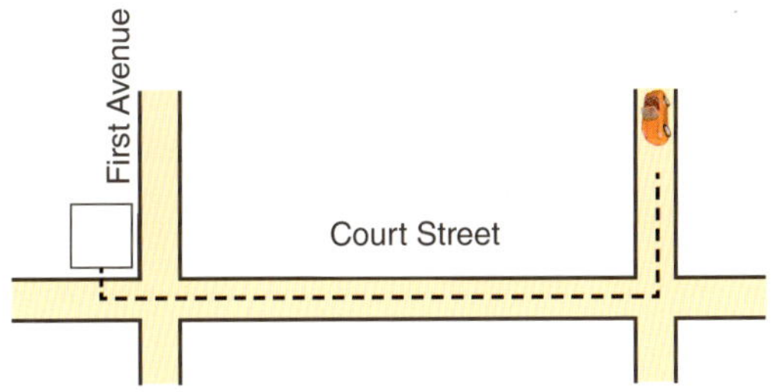

MIN CHUL: Uh-oh. I think we're running out of gas.

JAN: OK... where's the nearest gas station?

MIN CHUL: I don't know. Let's ask someone.

JAN: Excuse me.

MAN: Yes?

JAN: Is there a gas station near here?

MAN: Yes. Go straight and turn right on Court Street. Go one block. It's on the corner of Court Street and First Avenue.

JAN: Thanks!

B Practice the conversation in groups of three.

SPEAKING STRATEGY

Useful Expressions	
Asking for and giving directions	
Asking about a place in general	Excuse me. Is there a (gas station) near here? Yes. Go one block. There's one on the corner of (Court Street and First Avenue).
Asking about a specific place	Excuse me. Where's the (Bridge Theater)? It's on (Jay Street). Go straight and turn right (on Jay Street). It's in the middle of the block.
Speaking tip	
To start asking for directions, you can ask, *Are you familiar with this neighborhood / area?*	

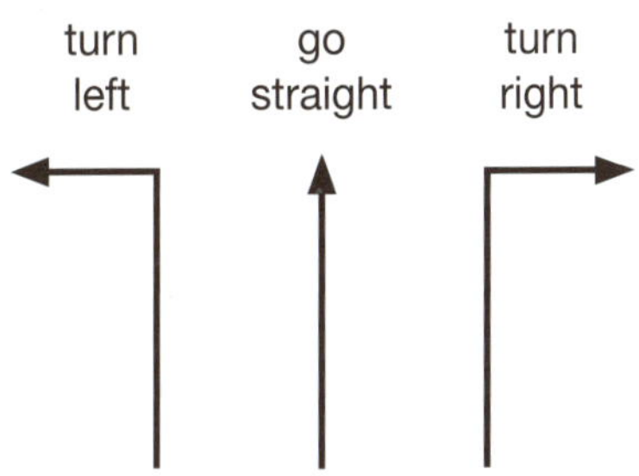

C Take turns asking a partner for directions to different places. Start at the X. Use the Useful Expressions to help you.

D With a partner, choose one place on the map and make a short conversation. Use the conversation at the top of the page as a model. Perform it for the class.

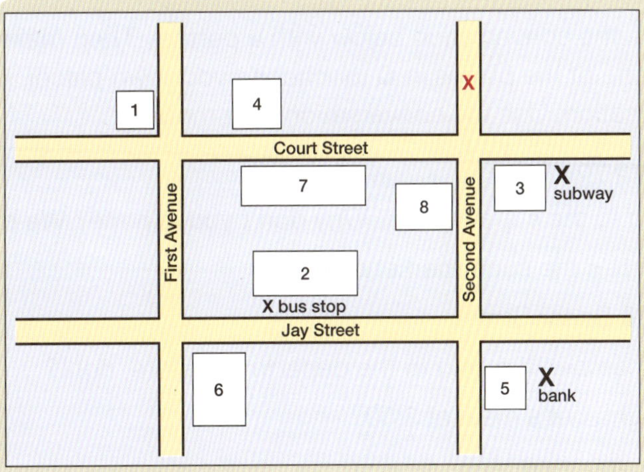

X Min Chul and Jan
1. gas station
2. Bridge Theater
3. Carl's Cafe
4. library
5. Pat's Hair Salon
6. grocery store
7. Jimmy's Gym
8. bookstore

5 GRAMMAR

at 2:00
on Spear Street
at 226 Spear Street
on the second floor

A Turn to page 229. Complete the exercises. Then do **B–D** below.

B Carla is a new student at Greenville College. Read the email to Carla. As you read, notice the **bold** words.

1. Underline the places mentioned in the email.
2. Work with a partner. Use the map on page 123 to find the places mentioned in the email.

Hi, Carla! Welcome to Greenville College!
Greenville is a small city. It's kind of boring, but it's very convenient.
Here are some important places you should know about:
The library is **across from** Jimmy's Gym.
The subway is **next** to Carl's Cafe.
The bus stop is **in front of** the Bridge Theater.
The bank is **behind** Pat's Hair Salon.
The bookstore is on Second Avenue, **between** Court Street and Jay Street.

C Look at the street scene below and answer the questions.

1. What's in front of the Mexican restaurant?
   ____
2. What's across from the theater?
   ____
3. What's behind the cafe?
   ____
4. What's next to the theater?
   ____
5. What's in front of the gym?
   ____
6. What's between the gym and the bank?
   ____

D Practice the conversation below with a partner. Then make a plan to meet at one of the places in **C** (or choose your own place). Create a new conversation. Use the conversation as a model.

A: Where are you now?
B: I'm going to the supermarket. Why don't you join me? We can shop together.
A: OK. Where's the supermarket exactly?
B: It's at 226 Spear Street.
A: Oh, I remember. It's next to the department store, right?
B: That's right. Let's meet at 2:00.
A: OK. See you then.

6 COMMUNICATION

A Read the information. Then answer the questions with a partner.

Ms. Smith and Ms. Jones live in the same apartment building at 50 Dean Street. They have tea together every Thursday afternoon at 4:00.

On this Thursday, Ms. Smith doesn't answer the doorbell. Ms. Jones calls Mr. Busby, the apartment manager. He has a key to Ms. Smith's apartment. He opens the door and sees Ms. Smith on the floor. She is dead!

Later, the police find an apartment key under Ms. Smith's sofa. The number on the key is 300. The key belongs to the killer.

1. Who are Ms. Smith and Ms. Jones?
2. Who is Mr. Busby?
3. What does Mr. Busby see?
4. What do the police find?
   Why is it important?

B Work with your partner to find the killer. Try to be the first in the class.

Partner A: Read the sentences to your partner.

Partner B: Write the names and room numbers on the doors.

Ms. Smith lives in apartment 305.

Mr. and Mrs. Busby live across from Ms. Smith.

Ms. Sanchez lives between Dr. Lewis and Mr. and Mrs. Busby.

Mr. Hu lives across from Ms. Sanchez.

The apartment next to Ms. Smith's is 303.

Mr. Hu lives next to Miss Jones.

Ms. Jones lives across from apartment 300.

Let's see. Ms. Smith lives in apartment 305.

Ms. Smith... 305... OK, got it.

LESSON B BIG CITIES

Cities with the world's worst traffic:
1. ____________
2. Istanbul, Turkey
3. Mexico City, Mexico

Traffic in Istanbul, Turkey

1 VOCABULARY

A Guess: Which city has the worst traffic? Check your answer at the bottom-right of the page.

B Read the information. Then take turns asking and answering the questions below with a partner.

The problem with traffic:	What can cities do?
• During **rush hour** (the busy times in the morning and evening), people are often **stuck in traffic**. Their cars don't move. In **heavy traffic**, a 30-minute trip is often an hour. • Having many cars on the road causes a lot of air **pollution**. Worldwide, air pollution kills over three million people every year.*	• At the moment, Jakarta, Istanbul, and Mexico City all have large **populations** of nine million people or more. But these cities don't have enough **public transportation** (buses, subways, and trains). Each city is trying to build more.

*Source: The World Health Organization

Word Bank

Opposites

a lot of ↔ a little (pollution) (*n.*)

very ↔ not very (polluted) (*adj.*)

heavy ↔ light (traffic)

1. When are people usually stuck in traffic?
2. In heavy traffic, how long is a 30-minute trip?
3. What causes air pollution?
4. What are the three cities above trying to do about traffic?
5. In your city, how is...

the traffic during rush hour?	heavy	so-so	light
the air?	very polluted	so-so	not very polluted
public transportation?	terrible	so-so	excellent

The traffic during rush hour is very heavy in Tokyo.

A. 1. Jakarta, Indonesia

2 LISTENING

A Answer the questions with a partner.

1. Look at the map. In what country is the state of Vermont?
2. Look at the photos. What things do you see?

B **Listen for context.** Listen. Circle the correct answer to complete the sentence. **Track 50**

You are listening to ______.

a. a news report
b. an advertisement
c. an interview
d. a class lecture

C **Listen for details.** Read the sentences. Then listen again and circle the correct words. **Track 50**

1. The state of Vermont is very polluted / not polluted at all.
2. Its capital city has a small / large population.
3. During rush hour in Vermont's capital city, most people are / aren't stuck in traffic.
4. Vermont is famous for its sweet maple syrup / ice cream.
5. Outside the capital city, there are a lot of things to do outdoors / indoors.

D Answer the questions with a partner.

1. Do you want to visit Vermont? Why or why not?
2. Is there an area in your country like Vermont? What is its population? What is it famous for? Do you like this place?

3 READING

A **Make predictions.** Look at the title, introduction, and photos. What do you think are some of the pros (good things) and cons (bad things) of living in these two cities? Tell your partner.

B **Read for details.** Work with a partner. Copy the chart into your notebook. Then:

Student A: Read about Lima.

Student B: Read about Hong Kong.

What does the reading say about your city? Complete the chart. Write *NG* if the information is not given.

	Lima	Hong Kong
weather		
public transportation		
traffic		
food		
neighborhoods		
pollution		
housing		
things to do outside the city		

C Tell your partner about your city in **B**. Your partner listens and takes notes.

D Choose a fact that is not given (NG) in the chart in **B**. Go online and find information about the topic. Add it to the chart.

E Answer the questions with a partner. Use information in the chart to explain.

1. Do you prefer Lima or Hong Kong? Why?
2. Compare your city to Lima or Hong Kong in three ways. How is your city the same or different?

There's heavy traffic in our city center, too.

Track 51

CITY LIVING

What are the pros and cons of living in different cities around the world? Today we focus on Lima and Hong Kong.

Plaza San Martin, Lima

Victoria Harbor, Hong Kong

When people think of Peru, they imagine rain forests, mountains, and Machu Picchu. These things are not in Lima, but this city is still a nice place to live and visit for several reasons. For one thing, many other cities in Latin America have hot, humid weather in the summers. But Lima doesn't. It has pleasant[1] weather all year (15° C / 59° F to 27° C / 81° F). Many of the city's older neighborhoods are beautiful and have small hotels, museums, clubs, and cafes. The Historic Center has some of the world's best colonial architecture, and there are even pre-Incan ruins.[2]

If you want to spend some time outside the city, it is easy to visit beaches, rain forests, and mountains near Lima. The city also has a lot of public transportation, but there's heavy traffic in the city center, especially during rush hour. Be careful walking or driving there!

[1]If the weather is *pleasant*, it is comfortable, not too hot or too cold.
[2]*Ruins* are the parts of an old building that are still standing. The *Inca* people had a very large empire; its center was in Peru.

Hong Kong—once a small fishing village— is an international business center and an interesting mix of East and West, old and new. Modern buildings are next to small temples. Popular nightclubs are close to traditional teahouses. Busy crowds fill the streets at all hours of the day, but outside the city, there are parks for walking or relaxing. Hong Kong is also famous for its delicious street food and its many excellent restaurants with food from all over Asia, Europe, and the Americas.

There are many great things about Hong Kong, but there are some problems, too. Housing isn't cheap. With a population of over seven million, it is one of the world's most expensive cities to live in. Also, the pollution in Hong Kong is not bad, but in the summer and winter, the air is sometimes polluted.

4 GRAMMAR

A Turn to page 230. Complete the exercises. Then do **B–D** below.

Questions and Answers with *How much / How many*		
	Count nouns	Noncount nouns
	How many parks are there in your city?	**How much** pollution is there?
Affirmative	(There are) **a lot** / **many**. **some** / **a few**. **two**.	(There's) **a lot**. **some** / **a little**.
Negative	There are**n't many**. / **Not many**. There are**n't any**. / **None**.	There is**n't much**. / **Not much**. There is**n't any**. / **None**.

B Complete the questions with *much* or *many*. Then think about your answers to the questions.

In your city…

1. how ________ people are there?
2. how ________ smog is there in the air today?
3. how ________ parks are there?
4. how ________ taxis are there?
5. how ________ noise is there?
6. how ________ crime is there?
7. how ________ fun things to do at night are there?
8. how ________ very cold days are there?
9. how ________ hot days are there?
10. how ________ traffic is there?

Word Bank
crime = illegal action
smog = air pollution

C Ask and answer the questions in **B** with a partner. Use the words in **bold** in the chart in your answer.

How many parks are there in your city?

Not many. Maybe two.

D In your opinion, is your city a good place to live? Why or why not? Use your answers in **C** to explain to a partner.

There aren't many parks in this city. We need more parks so people can relax and exercise.

Lumpini Park, Bangkok, Thailand

5 WRITING

A Read the brochure. This city wants to host the 2032 Summer Olympics. In your opinion, is it a good city?

B Imagine that your city wants to host the 2032 Summer Olympics. Make your own brochure with a partner.

1. Include this information about your city in your brochure:
   - the weather
   - public transportation
   - hotels and restaurants
   - airports and train stations
   - traffic
   - the amount of pollution
   - nightlife (clubs, theaters, concerts)
   - our idea: ______________
2. Think about how to organize the brochure.
   - How will you present the information?
   - What pictures will you use?

Remember to be positive! The class will choose the best brochure to represent your city.

PLEASANT VALLEY

wants to host the 2032 Summer Olympics!

Pleasant Valley has over 300 days of sun a year!

There are many great neighborhoods in **Pleasant Valley**.

The Downtown Area is the center of business and nightlife. Public transportation is excellent. There is a subway system. It connects to an international airport. There are also a lot of buses and cabs. It's easy to go everywhere.

The Northern District is famous for its hotels and restaurants.

South Beach has 20 kilometers of unpolluted beaches and a new sports stadium.

6 COMMUNICATION

A Present your brochures.

- **The presenters:** With your partner, present your brochure to the class. Each person should explain a part of the brochure.
- **The listeners:** For each presentation, complete these sentences on a piece of paper:

I liked ______ about this brochure.

I wanted to know more about ______.

I wanted to know more about the weather in summer. That's important for visitors.

B Look at your notes in **A**. Which brochure and presentation was the best? Why? Tell a partner.

C As a class, choose the best brochure.

MEMO

NATIONAL GEOGRAPHIC LEARNING

KEIMYUNG UNIVERSITY

NATIONAL GEOGRAPHIC LEARNING

MEMO

KEIMYUNG UNIVERSITY

9 ALL ABOUT YOU

Look at the photo. Answer the questions.

1. What are the people doing?
2. Can you do what they are doing?
3. What sports do you like to play?

UNIT GOALS

1. Talk about sports that you like and play
2. Invite and offer using *Do you want*
3. Describe different personalities
4. Talk about how often you do things

Photographers take photos of a surfer in Oahu, Hawaii, in the United States.

LESSON A SPORTS

A group of children do yoga outside.

1 VIDEO Yoga in Schools

A Look at the picture. Have you seen people do this before? Does it look fun? Tell a partner.

B You are going to watch a video about teaching yoga in school. Read the sentences. What do people say about yoga? Fill in the missing words.

1. "Sometimes it takes a lot of courage to just be a little bit more still and not ________."
2. "I forget about the ________ things that are happening."
3. "I feel ________ and calm."
4. "Before, I'm always just running around and not really paying attention, but after yoga, I feel, like ________ and can do my work faster."
5. "Yoga is simply a ________..."
6. "________% of our students say that after yoga class, they are more ready to learn."

C Look at your answers in **B**. Did the students enjoy their yoga class? Explain your answer to a partner.

D Is having a yoga class in your school a good idea? Why or why not? Tell your partner.

2 VOCABULARY

A The sports words in each column are missing the same vowel (*a, e, i, o,* or *u*). Fill in the missing letters. Work with a partner. Which words go with *play* or *do*? with *go*?

1. b__seb__ll

2. b__sketb__ll

3. volleyb__ll

4. b__dminton

5. sw__mm__ng

6. p__ng pong

7. surf__ng

8. sk__ __ng

9. y__ga

10. jud__

11. b__wling

12. j__gging

13. hock__y

14. t__nnis

15. socc__r

16. pilat__s

B Ask a partner these questions.

1. Can you play _____ well?
2. Name one person who does _____. Why are they good at it?
3. When was the last time you went _____? How was it?

Can you play volleyball well?

No, I can't. I'm too short!

play / do + noun
You **play** a game of *soccer, basketball,* etc.
Also with **play**: *cards, darts, golf, rugby*
You **do** martial arts (*judo, kickboxing,* etc.) and other activities. Also with **do**: *gymnastics, crafts, puzzles*

go + noun + *-ing*
You can often do activities with **go** alone. Also with **go**: *camping, climbing, fishing, golfing*

3 LISTENING

A **Use visual cues.** Look at the title in **B** and the photo at the bottom of the page. What is this listening about?

B **Make predictions.** Read the paragraph. Then listen and complete it. Answer the question below. Track 52

From Physician to Beach Bum

In the 1950s, Dorian "Doc" Paskowitz was a successful physician. He was handsome and in good health. To many people, Doc's life seemed perfect. But it wasn't. Doc was ____________. He didn't like his work. The one thing he loved was ____________. So one day, Doc decided to change his life. He decided to follow his ____________.

What do you think happened to Doc Paskowitz and his family? Circle your answer(s). Then explain your ideas to a partner.

a. He surfed all the time.
b. He became a doctor in another city.
c. He traveled with his family.
d. He built a house on the beach.

C **Listen for gist.** Listen to more of the story and complete the sentences. Track 53

1. Doc and his wife had ____________.
2. The family became a ____________.

D **Listen for details.** Listen to the rest of the story and choose the correct answer for each item. Track 54

1. They lived ________.
   a. in a small camper b. a busy life
2. They visited places like ________.
   a. California and Australia b. Mexico and Venezuela
3. The family had ________.
   a. a lot of money b. a small business
4. The children did not ________.
   a. go to school b. learn to surf well

WORLD LINK

Where are the best places in the world to go surfing? Research three locations online and report back to your class.

E What do you think of the Paskowitz family? Did they have a good life? Why or why not? Discuss with a partner.

4 SPEAKING

A Listen to the conversation. Underline Connie's offer. Circle Gina's invitation. **Track 55**

CONNIE: Hey, Gina. Do you want some ice cream?
GINA: No, thanks. I'm going out.
CONNIE: Really? Where are you going?
GINA: I'm going to play tennis. Do you want to come?
CONNIE: Sorry, I can't. I need to study.
GINA: Well, come later then. We're playing all afternoon.
CONNIE: It sounds nice... but I'm not very good at tennis.
GINA: Don't worry about that. You don't have to play. You can just watch. Come on, it'll be fun.
CONNIE: Well, OK. I'll see you in an hour.
GINA: OK, see you later... and maybe we can have some ice cream afterwards!

B Practice the conversation with a partner.

SPEAKING STRATEGY

C Complete the information below.

1. Sport or activity I like to do: ____________________
2. Place to do it: ____________________
3. Day / time to do it: ____________________

D Make a conversation with a partner. Use the conversation above and the Useful Expressions to help you. Follow the steps below.

1. Invite your partner to do your activity.
2. Your partner should first decline the invitation.
3. Next, your partner accepts it.
4. Switch roles and repeat.

E Perform one of your conversations for the class.

Useful Expressions	
Inviting and offering with *Do you want*	
Inviting	Do you want to come? [*want* + *to* + verb] Sure, I'd love to! Sorry, I can't. I'm busy. Um, no thanks. I'm not good at...
Offering	Do you want some ice cream? [*want* + noun] Yes, please. / Yes, thanks. No, thank you. / No, thanks. I'm fine.

Speaking tip

You can also use *would like* to invite: *Would you like to come with us?*

5 GRAMMAR

A Turn to page 231. Complete the exercise. Then do **B–D** below.

Verb + Infinitive	Verb + Noun
I **love** / **like** to play volleyball.	I **love** / **like** sports.
I **forgot** to explain the rules.	I **need** my uniform.

Verbs like *forget, hate, learn, like, love, need, decide, plan, prepare,* and *want* can be followed by a noun or the infinitive (*to* + the base form of the verb).

B **Pronunciation: Reduced *to*.** Listen and repeat. What do you notice about the pronunciation of the word *to* in each sentence? **Track 56**

1. I like to play golf.
2. She likes to go jogging.
3. I love to sleep late.
4. He hates to study.
5. We plan to fly to Paris.
6. Do you like to play chess?
7. I want to be early.
8. I hate to be late.

C This is Jenna. For each picture, make up a sentence about her or the people she's with. Use the verbs given.

D Ask and answer the questions with a partner.

What is one thing...

you love to do on the weekend?

you need to study harder?

you want to do by the end of the year?

What are two things...

you plan to do soon?

you want for your next birthday?

you like about your school?

What are two things you like about your school?

Let's see... I like my classmates. They're friendly. And I also like...

6 COMMUNICATION

A Read the questions below. Write your answers under *My answer* in the chart.

	My answer	Classmate's name	Classmate's answer
1. What's your favorite sport or event to watch?			
2. Which sport do you most like to play?			
3. Who's your favorite athlete?			
4. What do you want for your birthday?			
5. What movie do you want to see?			
6. What is one thing you learned in the last year?			
7. Where do you plan to go next year?			
8. What do you want to do this weekend?			

B For each question, interview a *different* classmate. Write each person's name and answer in the chart.

C Get into a group of three. For each question, read a classmate's answer. Do *not* say the person's name. Your group guesses which classmate gave that answer.

I asked the question, "What's your favorite sport or event to watch?" This person loves to watch soccer.

I know! That's Mateo.

Yes, that's right!

LESSON B PERSONALITY

Penny and Pearl are both friendly. They are also **bright** (intelligent). However, their friends say they are very different.

Penny is very **organized**. She knows where everything is in her apartment.

Penny is really **ambitious**. Someday, she wants to have her own company.

Penny's very **careful** with her money. In fact, she's a little bit **selfish**—sometimes she doesn't like to share.

Penny is somewhat **reserved**. She has two or three close friends and doesn't go out a lot.

Pearl's apartment is kind of **messy**: there are dirty dishes in the sink and magazines on the floor.

Pearl is very **laid-back** (relaxed) about life and work.

Sometimes Pearl is **careless** with money—she forgets to pay her bills.

But she's very **generous**. She will share anything with you.

Pearl is **talkative**. She talks to everyone and is comfortable at parties.

1 VOCABULARY

You can use these words to make adjectives stronger:
very organized **really** ambitious
You can use these words to weaken negative adjectives:
a little (bit) selfish **somewhat** reserved **kind of** messy

A Penny and Pearl are cousins. Read about their personalities. Then answer the questions with a partner.

1. Which words in **blue** are opposites?
2. Which words do you think are positive? Which are negative?

B Look at the pictures. Which items belong to Pearl? to Penny? How do you know? Write their names.

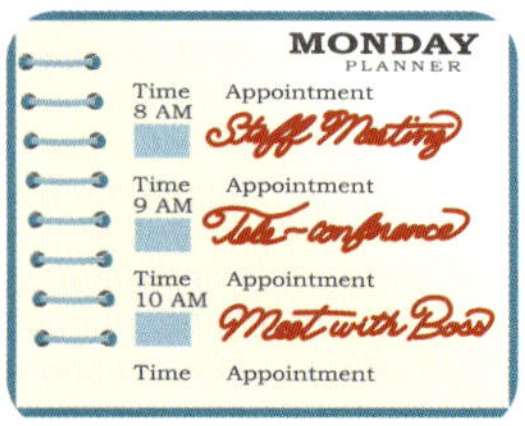

1. ______________

2. ______________

3. ______________

4. ______________

C Which words in blue do you think describe Penny? Which describe Pearl? Explain your answers to a partner.

A **competitive** person wants to be more successful than other people.

An **impulsive** person does things suddenly without thinking carefully.

A **creative** person has a lot of new ideas, especially in the arts (music, dance, etc.).

A **private** person doesn't like others to know how he or she feels.

D Is your personality more like Pearl's or Penny's? How? Tell a partner.

2 LISTENING

A **Use visual cues.** Look at the photos. What are the people doing? Guess: How do the people feel?

Word Bank
Opposites
patient ↔ impatient

B **Infer; Listen for gist.** A man is going to talk about two personality types: Type A and Type B. Listen and circle the correct answer. **Track 57**

1. The talk is happening at a company / hospital / school.
2. Photo 1 / Photo 2 / Both photos above show(s) a Type A person.

C **Listen for details.** Look up any unfamiliar words below. Then listen again. Which words describe a Type A person? Check (✓) them. **Track 57**

☐ angry ☐ laid-back ☐ patient
☐ competitive ☐ nervous ☐ a workaholic

D Answer the questions with a partner.

1. Guess: What words describe a Type B person? Make a list of your ideas.
2. Are you more Type A or Type B? Why?
3. "Being Type A can be bad for your health." Do you agree or disagree with this sentence? Why?

3 READING

A **Use background knowledge.** Look at the title of the reading and the four personality types. Do you know about any of the people in the photos? What do they do?

B **Make predictions.** Guess the answers about the four personality types. Sometimes more than one answer is possible.

This person...	The Dreamer	The Partner	The Thinker	The Artist
1. likes to follow rules.		✓		
2. is creative.				
3. listens to others' opinions.				
4. is a problem solver.				
5. has strong ideas about things.				
6. is careful.				
7. is organized and helpful.				
8. doesn't like change.				
9. does things without thinking carefully.				

C **Scan for information.** Look quickly at the reading to find the answers in **B**. Correct any incorrect answers.

D **Read for details.** Read the passage again. Which one or two of the personality types describe(s) you? your best friend? your parents? Why? Tell a partner.

I'm a mix of the Dreamer and the Artist.

WORLD LINK

Research one of the people talked about in the reading.

Does the personality type describe him or her? Why or why not?

LIFE STYLE

Track 58

Malala Yousafzai

The Dreamer

A Dreamer thinks there is a "right" way to do things. This person wants to live in the "perfect world." A Dreamer is often hardworking, organized, and very passionate[1] about his or her work. Many are good listeners and want to help others. Many Dreamers work as activists, lawyers, and in leadership roles.

[1]If you are *passionate* about something, you care about it a lot.

The Partner

A Partner wants to be in a group. For this person, rules and group harmony are important. Tradition is, too. Partners are often reserved, careful people, and change makes them nervous. Many do well as managers, police officers, and politicians.

Famous Partners: Queen Elizabeth II, former UN Secretary-General Ban Ki-Moon

Ban Ki-Moon

The Thinker

For Thinkers, understanding things is very important. They like to solve problems and make new things. Thinkers can also be competitive. They like to win. They are careful, ambitious people and often have very strong opinions. Many Thinkers work as scientists, inventors, politicians, and engineers.

Famous Thinkers: filmmaker and inventor James Cameron, scientist Stephen Hawking, businesswoman Sheryl Sandberg

Stephen Hawking

The Artist

Artists want to be free. They don't want to follow the rules all the time. Artists like action and are often impulsive. They also like trying new things, and they aren't afraid of change. Like Thinkers, many Artists have strong opinions. They do well in creative fields like music, acting, design, and in some sports.

Famous Artists: fashion designer Yang Li, soccer player Luis Suárez, singer Beyoncé

Beyoncé

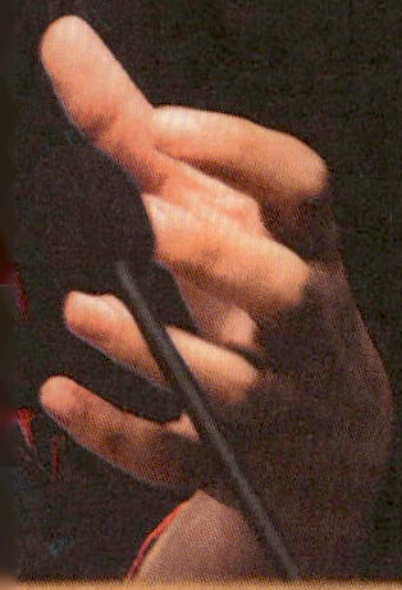

Famous Dreamers: activist Malala Yousafzai, lawyer Amal Ramzi Clooney, journalist and food activist Carlo Petrini

4 GRAMMAR

A Turn to page 231. Complete the exercises. Then do **B** and **C** below.

<table>
<tr><th colspan="4">How often...? Frequency Expressions</th></tr>
<tr><td rowspan="4">How often do you see your best friend?</td><td rowspan="3">(I see her)</td><td>every</td><td>day / Monday / week / month / summer.</td></tr>
<tr><td>once
twice
three times
several times</td><td>a day / a week / a month / a year.</td></tr>
<tr><td>all the time.
once in a while.</td><td rowspan="2"></td></tr>
<tr><td colspan="2">Hardly ever.</td></tr>
</table>

B Answer the questions about yourself.

How often do you…	Answer
1. go shopping and spend too much money?	I spend too much money once in a while.
2. watch TV?	______.
3. buy things for your friends or family?	______.
4. play video games and win?	______.
5. go on dates?	______.
6. text your friends?	______.
7. clean your desk?	______.
8. stay up late studying or working?	______.

C Take turns asking and answering the questions in **B** with a partner. Are you similar or different?

> I play games and win all the time. I'm really competitive.

> I only clean my desk once in a while. I'm kind of messy.

5 WRITING

A Read the student's personality profile. What adjectives does he use to describe himself? Circle them.

What are you like?

Usually, I'm kind of shy. For example, I like to go to parties, but it's hard to talk to new people. I feel nervous, so I'm kind of quiet. But once you get to know me, I'm really talkative. I like to tell jokes, and I'm very funny. I'm also a little competitive. I play video games with my friends all the time, and I hate to lose. For this reason, they hardly ever win!

B Think of three personality adjectives to describe yourself. Write them below. Also use one of the words given with the adjective.

I'm very / kind of / a little ______________________.

I'm very / kind of / a little ______________________.

I'm very / kind of / a little ______________________.

C Write about yourself. Remember to explain each idea in **B** with an example.

D Exchange your paper with a partner. Circle any mistakes. Then answer the question in **A** about your partner. Did you learn anything new about him or her? Tell the class.

6 COMMUNICATION

A Use the chart to interview a partner. Circle his or her answers.

Personality Quiz

Questions	Answers	
How often do you clean your room?	**a.** once a week	**b.** once in a while
How often do friends ask for your advice?	**a.** all the time	**b.** hardly ever
What is more important?	**a.** being kind	**b.** being honest
What is more important?	**a.** agreeing with the group	**b.** saying my opinion
Are you careful with money?	**a.** Yes, most of the time.	**b.** No, not really.
What is more important to you?	**a.** success	**b.** happiness
You're playing a game. Which sentence describes you?	**a.** I'm very competitive. I hate to lose.	**b.** I'm kind of laid-back. I want to win, but if I lose, it's OK.
Your cell phone isn't working. What do you do?	**a.** try to fix it myself	**b.** ask for help
What is more important?	**a.** facts	**b.** feelings
What do you want in your life?	**a.** many different experiences	**b.** the same job
What is more important?	**a.** being free	**b.** being careful
You get a free ticket to Paris. The plane leaves tomorrow. Do you go?	**a.** Yes! I'm very impulsive.	**b.** No way! That's too scary.

B Total your partner's points for each color (a = 2 points, b = 1 point). Read about the color(s) with the *most* points on page 237 and tell your partner about his or her personality type(s).

C Do you agree with your description? Explain your opinion to your partner.

MEMO

NATIONAL GEOGRAPHIC LEARNING

KEIMYUNG UNIVERSITY

MEMO

1 STORYBOARD

A Alexis and Peter are at a movie theater. Complete the conversation.

B Get into a group of three. Practice the conversation.

C Change roles and practice the conversation again.

2 SEE IT AND SAY IT

A Talk about the picture with a partner. Answer these questions.

- Where are these people?
- What are they doing?

Now answer these questions.

- How is the traffic and pollution in your city?
- How often do you take public transportation?
- What other forms of transportation do you take?
- Ask your partner one more question about the picture.

B With a partner, choose one pair of people in the picture. Role-play a conversation between the two people.

10 HEALTH

Look at the photo. Answer the questions.

1 What is this woman doing?

2 Is this activity good or bad for you? Why?

3 Imagine your friend wants to do this activity. Give one piece of advice.

UNIT GOALS

1 Identify parts of the body

2 Talk about health problems

3 Make requests and commands

4 Describe causes of stress and explain how to deal with them

Ultra trail runner Rory Bosio runs in Iceland's Lakagígar lava fields.

LESSON A THE BODY

Dr. Ellsworth Wareham mows his lawn.

1 VIDEO Centenarian's Guide to Longevity

A Read this information about Dr. Fraser and his study. What do you think Ellsworth Wareham does differently in his life? Discuss with a partner.

Dr. Gary Fraser studied 34,000 older people. He found that some people, like Dr. Ellsworth Wareham, were very healthy: they outlived other men by 9.5 years.

B Read the sentences and then watch the video about Dr. Wareham. Circle *T* for true and *F* for false.

1. Dr. Wareham retired at a young age. T F
2. Eating nuts and exercising are important for a healthy life. T F
3. Climbing stairs 40 times a week helps you to stay healthy. T F
4. Dr. Wareham lives a stressful life. T F
5. Dr. Wareham says, "You do the best you can." T F
6. Dr. Wareham says, "You can take control of your life." T F

C What do you think of Dr. Wareham's life and the advice in **B**? Tell a partner.

2 VOCABULARY

Ireen Wüst, speed skater

A With a partner, practice saying the words for parts of the body.

B Can you name each part of the body without looking at the words? Tell your partner.

C Close your books. Tell a partner things to do. Use body parts from the list.

Touch your nose.

Point to your right shoulder.

Stand on your left leg.

Word Bank

Opposites

broad ↔ **narrow** (shoulders)

long ↔ **short** (arms / legs)

big / **large** ↔ **little** / **small** (eyes / nose)

muscular (body / arms / legs)

WORLD LINK

Go online and learn more about Ireen Wüst. Where is she from? How many medals did she win? Why do you think she was successful?

3 LISTENING

A **Pronunciation: Vowel length with voiced and voiceless consonants.** Say the words. Then listen and repeat. How are the vowel sounds different in the group A and group B words? **Track 59**

A	B
bag	back
phase	face
feed	feet
made	mate
have	half
Ms.	Miss
save	safe

Vowels before voiced consonants are longer than those before voiceless ones.

B **Pronunciation: Vowel length with voiced and voiceless consonants.** Read the sentences. Then listen and repeat. Pay attention to the length of the vowel sound in the underlined words. **Track 60**

1. OK, Ms. Jones, where are you now?
2. I have a security camera in my home.
3. And please hurry! I don't feel safe.
4. Well, it's kind of dark. And I can only see his back.

C **Make predictions.** Before you listen, look at the photo and reread the sentences in **B**. What do you think the listening is going to be about? Discuss with a partner.

D **Listen for details.** Listen to the phone call and complete the information about the caller. **Track 61**

First name: ________________ Home address: ________________

Last name: ________________

E **Listen for details.** Listen. Circle your answer(s). **Track 62**

1. The caller is ______.
   a. at home b. calling the police c. worried
2. The man is ______.
   a. tall b. large c. young
3. The man ______.
   a. turns on the TV b. turns off the lights c. eats popcorn
4. In the end, the woman feels ______.
   a. worried b. scared c. embarrassed

F When there's an emergency (car accident, fire, etc.), people in the United States call 911. What number do you call? Have you ever called that number? Tell a partner.

4 SPEAKING

A Listen to the conversation. What's wrong with Jon? Check (✓) the box(es). **Track 63**

☐ His head hurts. ☐ His back hurts. ☐ He's tired.

MIA: Hello?

JON: Hi, Mia. It's Jon.

MIA: Jon! Where are you? It's 7:30. The movie starts in 20 minutes.

JON: Sorry to call so late, but I can't meet you tonight.

MIA: Really?

JON: Yeah, I don't feel well.

MIA: What's wrong?

JON: I have a headache, and I'm really tired.

MIA: Oh, sorry to hear that. Well, get some rest, and I'll call you in the morning.

JON: OK. Talk to you then.

B Practice the conversation with a partner.

SPEAKING STRATEGY

C What's wrong with Jenna? Match each pair of sentences to one picture.

1. She has a backache. Her back hurts.
2. She has a stomachache. Her stomach hurts.
3. She has a sore throat. Her throat hurts.
4. She has a fever and a bad cold. She has a temperature.

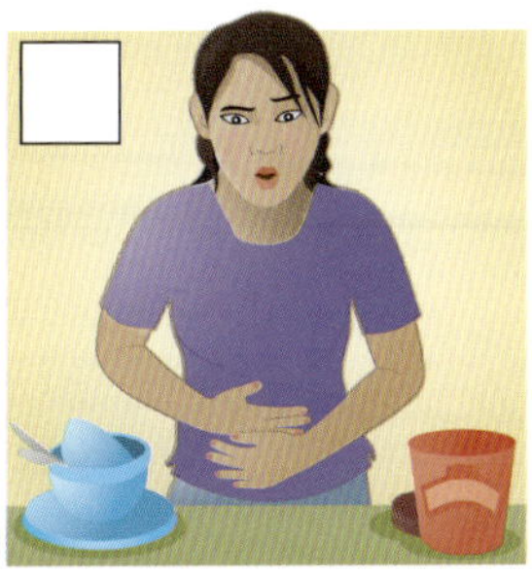

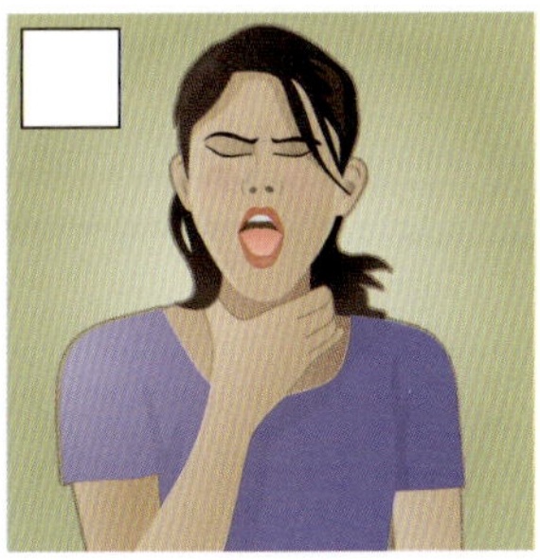

D With a partner, take turns practicing the conversation in **A** again. Then use the words you just learned in **C** to make a new conversation.

E Role-play with a partner. You have plans to meet a friend, but you don't feel well. Call your friend and explain the situation. Use the Useful Expressions to help you.

I'm sorry, but I can't go to the party. I have a bad cold.

Oh, no! I'm sorry to hear that. Get some rest!

Useful Expressions
Talking about health problems
What's wrong? / What's the matter? I don't feel well. I'm sick. I have a / an (fever). My (leg) hurts.
Speaking tip
When you hear bad news, you can respond with *(I'm) sorry to hear that.* or *Oh, that's too bad.*

F Change roles and practice again.

5 GRAMMAR

A Turn to page 232. Complete the exercise. Then do **B** and **C** below.

Imperatives		
Don't	**Base form**	
	Take	a break.
Don't	work	too hard.
	Get	some rest.

B Use the verbs in the box to complete the health tips. Use affirmative or negative forms of the imperative. You will use one word in the box twice.

drink	eat	give	go	sleep	take	wash

Health tips: The common cold

To stay healthy:

1. ___Take___ vitamins.
2. ___Don't eat___ a lot of junk food.
3. ____________ for 8–9 hours a night.
4. ____________ your hands often.
5. ____________ a cup of green tea daily.
6. ____________ too much soda. Water is better.

If you have a cold:

7. ____________ to school or work.
8. ____________ an aspirin for pain and fever.
9. ____________ aspirin to children under 12! It's dangerous.
10. ____________ a bowl of chicken soup.

C Work with a partner. Read the list and add your own idea to it. Then imagine you have one of these health problems. Ask your partner for advice.

1. I can't sleep at night.
2. I have a stomachache.
3. My legs hurt after I run.
4. Your idea: ____________

I can't sleep at night.

Don't drink coffee in the evening!

Exercise helps you stay healthy, too.

6 COMMUNICATION

A This poster gives advice. Read it and then answer the questions.

1. Have you ever seen a poster like this?
2. Where do you see posters like this in your city?
3. What does the poster tell people to do?
4. What other ideas can you add to the poster?

B Read the ideas for poster titles. With a partner, write another idea.

Fight pollution in our city!
Eat healthy, live longer.
Get in shape today!
Protect your skin this summer!
Don't drink and drive.
Your idea: ______________

C Use one of the titles from **B** to create a poster on a separate piece of paper. Think of what advice to give.

D **Group A:** Present your poster to another pair. Discuss it with them.
Group B: What do you like most about the poster? Can you add one piece of advice to the poster?
Change roles and repeat.

LESSON B STRESS

ZOE: I'm **stressed**. I have three exams and two papers to write this month. I don't **have time** to do it all and I have no time to **relax**!

MIGUEL: I have a **stressful** job, and I work long hours. In the past, I was **full of energy**. But now, I'm always **low on energy** and tired, so I drink a lot of coffee. Then I can't sleep at night.

1 VOCABULARY

Word Bank

Opposites

be full of ↔ be low on (energy)

stressed ↔ relaxed

stressful ↔ relaxing

A Work with a partner. Answer the questions.

1. Find the word *stress* in your dictionary. Is stress good or bad?
2. Why is each person above stressed?

B What can each person do? Match the ideas (a–d) with a person. Some ideas might match both people. Explain your ideas with your partner.

To **deal with** stress, Zoe / Miguel should…

a. **reduce** (lower) the amount of coffee he or she drinks.
b. **take time** to relax every day.
c. **make a schedule** and do some work every day.
d. exercise more.

Miguel should exercise more. Exercise reduces stress and gives you energy.

C Are the sentences below true for you? Tell your partner.

1. Usually, I'm full of energy.
2. Usually, I have time to do all my work.
3. School or work is stressful for me.
4. To reduce stress, I listen to music.

2 LISTENING

A Look at the photos. Do you ever drink or take these things? If yes, how often?

Word Bank
You *drink* liquids like water.
You *take* vitamins / aspirin / medicine.

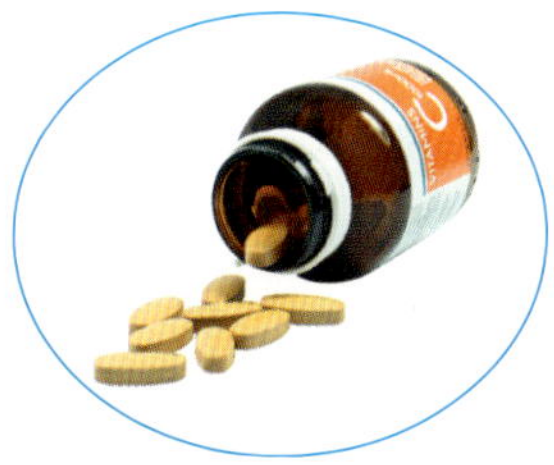

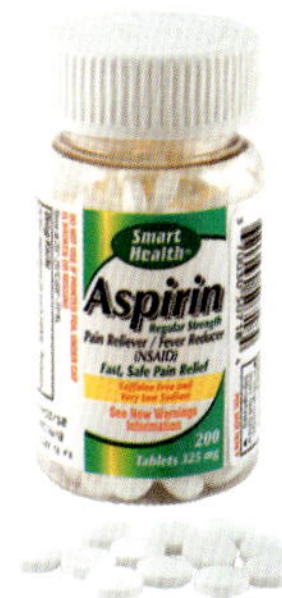

B **Listen for gist.** What is the advertisement about? Listen and circle the correct photo above. **Track 64**

C **Listen for details.** Read the sentences. Then listen and complete each blank with one or two words. **Track 65**

One person's opinion about the item

1. "Before I took _______________, I was living an _______________ life."
2. "I felt _______________ all the time."
3. "Now I'm _______________ energy, and I can deal with _______________ better."
4. "I _______________ these… and you will, too!"

More information about the item

5. They are selling _______________.
6. They cost $ ______.95.

D **Draw conclusions.** Look at your answers in **B** and **C**. Would you buy this product? Why or why not? Tell a partner.

E Role-play. Imagine you are low on energy. Your partner gives you some advice.

A: Hey, Marta, what's the matter?
B: Oh, I'm kind of low on energy.
A: That's too bad. Why?
B: I'm always sitting and studying in the library. I don't exercise.
A: Well, I have an idea…

3 READING

A **Make predictions.** Read the title and the first paragraph.

1. What is the student's problem?
2. What can the student do? Make a list of some ideas.
3. Read the entire passage and check your answers in 2.

B **Read for main ideas.** Write each sentence below in the correct place in the reading (1, 2, 3, or 4).

Eat well.	Get a study partner.
Don't do too much.	Stop and relax.

C **Infer meaning.** Find the phrases in italics in the reading. Complete each sentence.

1. Tip #1: If you *wait until the last minute*, you do something early / very late.
2. Tip #2: If you *take a break*, you stop / keep working for a short time.
3. Tip #4: If you are *under pressure*, you're feeling very stressed / relaxed.

D **Understand a writer's opinion.** Which sentences would the writer of the tips agree with? Check (✓) them. Explain your answers to a partner.

- ☐ It's best to study a little bit each day.
- ☐ The best hours for studying are from 11 PM to 1 AM.
- ☐ Breaks are good, but it's best to stay indoors.
- ☐ Drinking coffee helps you remember information better.
- ☐ It's good to tell a study partner your feelings.

E Talk with a partner. Do you agree with the study tips in the reading? Why or why not? Do you ever do these things?

HOW TO DEAL WITH STUDY STRESS

Track 66

I'm getting ready to take the university entrance exam. To prepare, I'm studying six hours a day. I want to do well, but I'm really stressed these days. I can't sleep. What can I do?

1. ____________________ Don't wait until the last minute, or just a day or two before the exam. Make a study schedule for yourself, but don't study too much in one day. You remember more by studying one hour each day for six days than six hours in one day. Also, don't study late at night. We often forget information studied then.
2. ____________________ You learn best when you study for two hours and then stop. Every hour, take a break for 10 to 15 minutes. Go for a walk. Exercise is a great way to reduce stress.
3. ____________________ Don't eat a lot of sugar or drink beverages with a lot of caffeine, like coffee or energy drinks. Eat foods high in vitamin B (for example, eggs, yogurt, green vegetables, tofu, and rice). These things give you energy and help you think better.
4. ____________________ A study partner can help you practice for the test. When you're under pressure and nervous about the exam, you can talk to your partner. This can reduce stress, too.

People study and read at the British Library, London, England.

4 GRAMMAR

A Turn to page 233. Complete the exercises. Then do **B** and **C** below.

When Clauses	
***When* clause**	**Result clause**
When(ever) I drink coffee,	I can't sleep.
Result clause	***When* clause**
I can't sleep	when(ever) I drink coffee.

B Complete the sentences with your own information.

1. When I don't feel well, I take aspirin and drink tea.
2. When I meet new people, ______.
3. When I don't understand something in English, ______.
4. When I have a lot to do, I ______.
5. When I (don't) take time to ______, I ______.
6. I get impatient when ______.
7. I feel happy when ______.
8. I feel ______ when ______.

C Take turns saying the sentences in **B**. For each sentence, your partner asks you one question.

When I don't feel well, I take aspirin and drink tea.

Really? Does it help?

5 WRITING

A Read about a student's problem and one person's advice. Answer the questions.

1. What is the student stressed about? Why is he stressed?
2. What advice does the other person give? Is it good advice?

Q: *I feel stressed when I think about graduation. I'm a senior in college. Soon, I have to get a job. When I think about that, I feel nervous. What can I do?*

A: When you feel stressed, try these two things: First, make a list of your goals. What do you want to do in the future? Write three ideas. Then talk to Ms. Kim, the school counselor. Show her your goals. She can give you some job advice. She can also help you plan for the future. Try these two things. They can reduce your stress.

B Read the list of stressful situations in the box and choose one. Write your sentence on a piece of paper. Explain why the situation is stressful for you.

> **I feel stressed when...**
> - I have to take a test.
> - I speak in English.
> - I have a lot to do and no time.
> - my idea: ____________

C Exchange papers with a partner.

1. Read your partner's problem.
2. What can your partner do? Write a reply.
   Give two pieces of advice. Use the example in **A** to help you.

D Give your reply to your partner. Read his or her ideas for your problem. Are they helpful?

6 COMMUNICATION

A Choose a situation below and make a one-minute role play about it with a partner. Use at least two *when* clauses in your conversation.

Student A: Explain your problem.

You...

- had a fight with a friend.
- have a lot of homework but don't have time to do it all.
- are under a lot of pressure at work.
- like a guy or girl, but you're nervous to talk to the person.

Student B: Give your partner some advice.

I have too much work. When it's time to go, I still have so much to do!

Really? Maybe you should talk to your boss.

When I do...

B Perform your role play for another pair. When you listen, answer these questions.

1. Why is the person stressed?
2. What advice did his or her partner give?
3. Is it good advice?
4. Can you think of other advice?

C Repeat **A** and **B**. This time, choose a new situation and change roles.

MEMO

NATIONAL GEOGRAPHIC LEARNING

MEMO

11 JOBS

Look at the photo. Answer the questions.

1 What is the man's job?

2 Is this job hard or easy?

3 Do you want to do a job like this? Why or why not?

UNIT GOALS

1 Identify and describe jobs

2 Talk about where you work and who you work for

3 Describe your work goals

4 Talk about things you can and can't do

A blacksmith demonstrates his metal work, Memphis, the United States.

LESSON A WHAT DO YOU DO?

A stunt pilot doing a trick. Would you want to do this job?

1 VIDEO Career Day

A Look at the jobs below. Which do you know? Look up the ones you don't know in a dictionary.

☐ a doctor	☐ a surfer	☐ a veterinarian	☐ the president
☐ an actress	☐ a pilot	☐ a lawyer	☐ a musician
☐ a web designer	☐ a photographer	☐ a filmmaker	☐ a baseball player

B Watch the video with the sound off. Guess: What jobs do the students want to do? Check (✓) your answers in **A**.

C Watch the video with the sound on. Check your answers in **B**.

D Choose the job you want to do in **A**. Tell a partner.

I want to be a pilot. It's an exciting job.

2 VOCABULARY

A Look at the pictures below. Then follow these instructions:

- Cover the chart and look at the pictures. Can you name any of the jobs?
- Check your answers. Practice saying the jobs with a partner.

He's a doctor.

Nouns ending in *-er* / *-or* or *-ist* often describe a job or something a person does.			
-er / -or	1. **doctor** 4. **telemarketer**	2. **web designer** 5. **police officer**	3. **programmer** 6. **lawyer**
-ist	7. **receptionist**	8. **hairstylist**	
person	9. **businessperson**	10. **delivery person**	
other	11. **flight attendant**	12. **nurse**	

B Look at the jobs in **A**. Answer the questions with a partner.

1. Which jobs make the most money?
2. Which jobs are easy? Which ones are hard?
3. Do you know anyone with these jobs?

3 LISTENING

A In your country, do students ever go to school *and* work? Discuss with a partner.

B **Listen for details.** Yana is a student. She is looking for a job. Read the question below. Then listen and circle the correct answer. **Track 67**

When can Yana work?

a. on some weekdays and all weekend
b. on some weekdays but not on the weekend
c. only on Saturdays and Sundays

Word Bank

Word partnerships with *job*

look for / get / have / find a job
a **part-time** / a **full-time** job

C **Listen for details.** Listen and complete the information about each job. **Track 68**

Jobs		
Job 1: a waitress at the Sunflower ______	Job 2: a tutor at the ______	Job 3: a cashier in a ______ store
Days/hours: from ______ to ______ in the ______	Days/hours: ______ or ______	Days/hours: on ______ from ______ to ______

D **Draw conclusions.** Look at your answers in **B** and **C**. Which jobs are good for Yana? Why? Tell a partner.

Word Bank

cashier = the person who gives and receives money at a store

tutor = a teacher for one student

waiter / waitress = someone who brings food and takes orders at a restaurant

E Read this list of different places to work. Where do you want to work? Rate the places from 1 (like a lot) to 6 (don't like very much). Tell a partner.

_____ in a cafe
_____ at school
_____ in a clothing store
_____ at home
_____ in an office
_____ outdoors

4 SPEAKING

A Valentina and Brad are at Ramon's party. Listen to their conversation. Then answer the questions. **Track 69**

1. What does Valentina do? (What's her job?)
2. Does she like her job? Why or why not?

VALENTINA: Hi, are you a friend of Ramon's?

BRAD: Yeah, hi. My name is Brad.

VALENTINA: Hi, Brad. I'm Valentina.

BRAD: Valentina... I know you.... You're Ramon's friend, too, right? You're a chef at that restaurant, The Boulevard....

VALENTINA: Yeah, that's me. But I'm not a chef anymore.

BRAD: Really? What do you do now?

VALENTINA: I work for a company called The Olive Kitchen. It imports food from Italy, Greece, and Turkey.

BRAD: Wow, what's that like?

VALENTINA: It's great. I travel, meet interesting people, and eat good food!

B Practice the conversation with a partner.

C **Pronunciation: Reduced words.** Work with a partner. Practice saying these two questions. Then listen and repeat. **Track 70**

What do you do? Where do you work?

D **Pronunciation: Reduced words.** Listen and fill in the missing words. Then practice the dialogs with a partner. **Track 71**

A: What do you do?
B: I'm a ________.
A: Where do you work?
B: In a ________ downtown.

A: What do you do?
B: I'm a ________.
A: Where do you work?
B: In a large ________.

In spoken English, small words like *do* and *you* are often reduced. Reduced forms are short. They sound different.

In questions, *do* is reduced from /du/ to /də/

SPEAKING STRATEGY

E Use the Useful Expressions to complete the dialogs below. Then read the dialogs with a partner.

1. A: So, what ________ do?
   B: I ________ Apple. ________ a programmer.
2. A: What ________ your parents ________?
   B: My mom works ________ a bank. My dad works ________ Samsung.

Useful Expressions

Talking about jobs

What do you / does she do?
- I'm a student. / She's a nurse.
- I work for myself. / She works for Telefonica.
- I work in / She works in a hospital / an office / a cafe.

F Create a new dialog with a partner. Use a job that you'd like to do. Then change roles and repeat.

5 GRAMMAR

A Turn to page 234. Complete the exercise. Then do **B–D** below.

Questions with *like*	
1. A: My mom works in a hospital.	2. A: My coworker is from Brazil.
B: Really? **What's** that **like**?	B: Oh? **What's** he **like**?
A: It's hard, but she enjoys it.	A: He's really nice.

B Read the two dialogs in the chart above. Pay attention to the questions. Which question asks about an experience? Which question asks about a person?

C What are the jobs below like? Take turns talking about each job with a partner. Use the words in the chart to help you.

1. police officer
2. pilot
3. flight attendant
4. telemarketer
5. delivery person
6. your idea: ____________

What's a delivery person's job like?

It's exciting.

Words to describe experiences	Words to describe people	
fun / exciting / cool / interesting ↔ boring safe ↔ dangerous easy ↔ hard	friendly / nice ↔ unfriendly fun ↔ serious hardworking ↔ lazy	cool / interesting ↔ boring shy ↔ outgoing strict ↔ easygoing

D What are these people like? Take turns talking about the people with a partner. Use the words from the chart in **C** to help you.

1. you
2. your classmates or coworkers
3. your parents

What are you like?

I think I'm a friendly person....

Some delivery people in cities use bikes to get around. It's a dangerous job!

6 COMMUNICATION

A Practice the conversation with a partner. Then answer the questions about Elena. What does she do? Who does she work for? What's her job like?

KURT: So, what do you do, Elena?

ELENA: I'm a reporter. I work for a music show called *Que Colores*. Here's my card.

KURT: Oh, thanks. So, what's your job like?

ELENA: It's fun. I meet different artists and go to concerts and film festivals.

KURT: That's cool!

Word Bank
reporter = someone who gets stories for the news

B Think of your dream job. Make three identical business cards on three pieces of paper. Then answer the questions below about your job. Use the model above.

	Me	Partner 1	Partner 2	Partner 3
What do you do?				
Who do you work for?				
What's your job like?				

C Imagine you are at a party. Introduce yourself to three people. Give each person your business card. Then complete the chart in **B** with information about each person you meet.

D Which person has the most interesting job? Tell the class.

LESSON B GETTING A JOB

This summer, I'm **doing an internship** at a fashion-design company. I work **part-time** (ten hours a week). I don't **make** any **money**, but I'm **getting** a lot of **experience**. In the future, maybe I can **get a full-time job** with this company. That's my **goal**.

1 VOCABULARY

A Read about Philippe's work goals. Tell a partner which things are true. Philippe...

1. works 40 hours a week.
2. works for free.
3. is learning to do a job.
4. has two jobs.
5. wants to work at the same place in the future.
6. wants to make money in the future.

> **Word Bank**
> *goal* = something you want to do in the future

Philippe doesn't work 40 hours a week. He works part-time.

B Complete the sentences with your ideas.

My work goals (in the future)	
1. I want to get... ☐ a full-time job. ☐ a part-time job. ☐ a different job. ☐ some work experience.	2. I want to work in / for ______. I want to do an internship at ______. 3. Pay: I want to make ______ a year / an hour.

C Tell a partner your answers in **B**. Are your goals the same?

I want to get a part-time job this summer.

In the future, I want to make $60,000 a year.

2 LISTENING

A **Make predictions.** Look up the words in the box. Then look at two students' summer jobs below. Answer the questions with a partner.

1. Where do Yuko and Davi work? What do they do?
2. Guess: What are their job responsibilities and requirements?

coach	tour guide
requirement	volunteer
responsibility	

Name: Yuko Abe **Age:** 21 **From:** Japan	**Name:** Davi Santos **Age:** 22 **From:** Brazil
Tour guide, Tokyo Disneyland	**Soccer coach, Madagascar**
Job responsibilities:	**Job responsibilities:**
• ________ people to the park	• Teach ________ to play soccer
• Answer ________ about where to go	
Job requirements:	**Job requirements:**
• Speak ________ and basic ________	• Be able to play ________
	• Speak some ________ or ________
Pay: ________ yen per month	**Pay:** ________

B **Listen for details.** Write a word or number in each blank in **A**. **Track 72**

C **Listen for a speaker's attitude.** Listen again. Circle the correct word in the first column. Then complete each word in the second. **Track 72**

Word Bank

Large numbers

1,000	one thousand
10,000	ten thousand
100,000	one hundred thousand
1,000,000	one million

Do they like their jobs?	Why?
1. Yuko likes / doesn't like her job.	The job is f________. She meets people from all over J________ and the w________
2. Davi likes / doesn't like his job.	The kids are g________, the country is b________, and he's l________ a lot.

D Are Yuko's and Davi's jobs interesting to you? Why or why not? Tell a partner.

I like Yuko's job. You can get experience and make some money. And it's a fun place to work.

3 READING

A **Make predictions.** Look at the title and photos on the next page. Guess: What does Michelle Phan do? Use ideas from the box.

a. department store cashier
b. waitress
c. model
d. businessperson
e. makeup artist

B **Read for details.** Read the article. Then complete the sentences with the jobs (a–e) from **A**. Two answers are extra.

1. In college, Michelle Phan was a(n) ______________________.
2. Today, she's a(n) ______________.

C **Scan for information.** Ask and answer the questions with a partner. Find the answers quickly in the reading.

1. What do Michelle Phan's videos teach people?
2. How many people watch her videos?
3. Why is she popular?
4. How much money does she make a year?
5. In the future, what is her goal?

D Answer the questions with a partner.

1. Name another entrepreneur. What does he or she do?
2. Do you have a hobby? Can you make money doing it? How?

An *entrepreneur* is a businessperson. Usually, he or she starts a new company.

Michelle Phan has one of the most popular channels on YouTube. Her videos teach people to put on makeup. A billion people have watched them.

Why is Phan so popular? She knows about makeup, of course. She also gives people helpful tips (what makeup to buy, how to look good with very little money, and many other ideas). But there's another reason: Phan is a regular[1] person, not a perfect model in a magazine. People watch her videos and they think, "I can look like her."

In addition to her YouTube channel, Phan now has her own makeup business (called "ipsy") and a line of makeup called "em." She also wrote a book and started a music business. In the future, she wants to start a new business, maybe in lifestyle or food.

Michelle Phan's work history:

- As a college student, she works as a waitress.
- She tries to get a job in a department store selling makeup, but she can't. She has no experience.
- In college, she starts making videos about makeup as a hobby.[2] Soon, thousands of people are watching them on YouTube.
- By age 27, she has a very popular channel and owns her own company. The company makes millions of dollars every year.

[1] A *regular* person is very similar to others.

[2] A *hobby* is something you do for fun.

YouTube entrepreneur Michelle Phan

Different types of makeup

4 GRAMMAR

A Turn to page 235. Complete the exercises. Then do **B–E** below.

Talking about Ability with *can / can't*		
***Yes / No* questions**	**Can** you speak French?	Yes, I **can**. / No, I **can't**.
***Wh-* questions**	Which languages **can** Carla speak?	(She **can** speak) Spanish and English.
	Who **can** speak Japanese?	Toshi (**can**).

B Read the job ad. Then complete the interview questions below. Write three *Yes / No* and two *Wh-* questions with *can.*

WANTED: Tour guide

Vacation hotel in beautiful Bali needs hardworking, friendly tour guides this summer.

Your job: Lead groups of people to areas of interest around the island.

Please be able to...
- speak English and one other language.
- drive a car.

Hours: Work full-time Monday - Saturday

***Yes / No* question**

1a. Can you work in Bali this summer?

2a. Can ______________ English?

3a. ______________ another language?

4a. __________________________?

Follow-up *Wh-* question

1b. When can you start?

2b. How well can you speak it?

3b. What other language ______________?

4b. __________________________?

C Ask a partner the interview questions in **B**. Is your partner a good person for the job?

Can you work in Bali this summer?

Yes, I can.

When can you start?

In June.

D Think of a job and make a new ad with your partner. Then write four or five interview questions with *can.*

E Get together with another pair.

1. Show them your job ad and questions. Read theirs.
2. Use your questions and interview one person from the other pair for your job. Your partner does the same. Take notes on the person's answers.
3. Compare notes with your partner. Which person is best for your job? Why?

5 WRITING

A Read the paragraph. Answer the questions with a partner.

1. What can he do well?
2. What are his goals? What does he want to be?

My work goals

I like comics and I can draw well. I usually draw my own characters. I practice every day. Right now, I'm majoring in digital art. In the future, I want to be a video game designer. Maybe I can do an internship first. Then I can get a full-time job and work for a big animation company. That's my goal.

B Write about your work goals. Answer the questions in **A** about yourself. Exchange papers with a partner. Answer the questions in **A** about your partner. Correct any mistakes.

6 COMMUNICATION

A Read the questions in the chart. Think about your answers.

Can you...

☐ speak and write well in your first language? ☐ remember phone numbers and names easily? ☐ tell interesting stories? Group 1 Total: ________	☐ play a musical instrument? ☐ read or write music? ☐ sing well? Group 3 Total: ________	☐ exercise for 30 minutes a day? ☐ play a sport well? ☐ dance well? Group 5 Total: ________
☐ solve problems quickly? ☐ play chess well? ☐ do math quickly in your head? Group 2 Total: ________	☐ fix or make things? ☐ draw or paint well? ☐ follow directions on a map? Group 4 Total: ________	☐ give good advice? ☐ talk to new people easily? ☐ understand others' feelings? Group 6 Total: ________

B Ask a partner the questions in the chart. Use *Can you....* For your partner's answers, write a number:

3 = Yes, I can. 2 = Yes, a little. 1 = No, I can't.

Can you play a musical instrument?

Yes, I can.

C Now add the points for each group and write the totals. Look at the chart below. What are good jobs for your partner?

7–9 points in...	Good jobs for you:
Group 1	teacher, lawyer, writer, salesperson, actor
Group 2	businessperson, programmer, doctor
Group 3	musician, DJ, singer

7–9 points in...	Good jobs for you:
Group 4	web designer, fashion designer, photographer, engineer
Group 5	dancer, athlete, coach
Group 6	teacher, manager, salesperson

D Look again at the chart in **A**. When did your partner say, "Yes, I can"? Ask your partner questions about these abilities.

What instrument can you play?

I can play the violin.

MEMO

MEMO

12 AT THE MOVIES

A captive audience watches a movie in 4-D in Baghdad, Iraq.

Look at the photo. Answer the questions.

1. Where are these people?
2. What kind of movie are they watching?
3. Complete this sentence:
   The last movie I saw was ______.
   Where did you watch the movie? Was the movie good?

UNIT GOALS

1. Talk about types of movies and your favorite film
2. Describe and rate movies
3. Tell someone about your future plans
4. Take and leave messages on the phone

1 VIDEO Spider-Man in Real Life

A Look at the photo. Do you know this character? What does he do?

B A group of people are creating a Spider-Man movie scene in real life. They are on top of a tall building in New York City.

1. Read the sentences below. Put the events in order from 1–6.
2. Watch the video and check your answers.

___ People on the street see Spider-Man.
___ Spider-Man jumps off the building.
___ The woman thanks Spider-Man.
___ Spider-Man and the woman fly away together.
___ Spider-Man fights the bad guy.
___ A woman needs help.

C Read the sentences. Then watch again and circle the best answer(s). Sometimes more than one answer is possible.

1. When the people on the street see the woman, they are excited / happy / worried.
2. When Spider-Man jumps off the building, the people on the street are shocked / scared / happy.
3. When Spider-Man flies away, the people on the street are worried / happy / confused.

D Do you know any Spider-Man movies? Do you like them? Why or why not? Tell a partner.

2 VOCABULARY

A Talk with a partner. Answer the questions.

1. Look at the movie posters. Practice saying each type of movie. What is your favorite kind of movie? Why?
2. Read about each one. Which one do you want to see? Why?
3. Which kinds of movies **make you** laugh? cry? think? scream?
4. Do you prefer a movie with a happy ending? Why or why not?

musical / drama
Four young men come together and create a singing group…

romantic comedy
At first, Rosie and Alex were friends…

action movie
James Bond fights the bad guys…

science fiction thriller
The Robinson family is in outer space and needs to get home…

horror film
A teenager has a strange new neighbor…

classic / old movie
A young woman living in New York meets a writer in her building and…

3 LISTENING

A **Pronunciation: Syllable stress.** Say the words. Then listen and repeat. Which syllable is stressed in each one? Underline it. **Track 74**

romantic   comedy   documentary   musical

B **Make predictions.** The words on the left describe movies. What do you think they mean? Discuss with a partner.

1. tearjerker
2. chick flick
3. blockbuster
4. indie

a. a successful movie that costs a lot to make
b. a less famous movie that costs less to make
c. a movie that makes you cry
d. a scary movie that is not good for children
e. a romantic movie that is popular with women

C **Check predictions.** Listen to a man and woman discuss movies. Match the words above to their definitions. One definition is extra. **Track 75**

D **Listen for details.** Listen again. How do the man and woman talk about likes and dislikes? Complete the sentences. **Track 75**

1. "I'm ________________ movies about love and romance."
2. "I thought you were ________________ action movies!"
3. "Sorry, but I'm ________________ horror films either."

Word Bank

Talking about likes and dislikes

(not) crazy about   *(not) a big fan of*   *(not) into*

E Complete the chart with one example of each type of movie. Then compare your list with a partner's. Tell your partner about one of the movies from your list.

tearjerker	
chick flick	
blockbuster	
indie	

At film festivals, like Sundance, reviewers and fans have the chance to see many movies in one place.

4 SPEAKING

A Listen to the conversation. Take a phone message for Michael. Complete the information in the box. **Track 76**

PAM: Hello?
SILVIO: Hi. Is Michael there, please?
PAM: Who's calling?
SILVIO: This is Silvio, a friend from school.
PAM: OK. Hang on a minute.
SILVIO: Thanks.
PAM: Hello? Sorry. Michael's not here. Can I take a message?
SILVIO: Yeah. We're going to a movie tonight. I have an extra ticket for Michael.
PAM: OK. What time does it start?
SILVIO: In a half hour from now—at 8:00.
PAM: All right. I'll give him the message.
SILVIO: Thanks a lot.

While You Were Out

Time of Call: ______________

______________ called.

Movie is at ______________. He has ______________ for you.

B Practice the conversation with a partner.

Word Bank

hang on = please wait

SPEAKING STRATEGY

C Think of a movie that you want to see with a friend. Then answer the questions to complete the chart.

What is the name of the movie?	Time	Place	What is your friend's name?

Useful Expressions

Taking and leaving a message

Hello? Is Michael there?
Who's calling, please?
This is Silvio.
OK. Hang on a minute.
Sorry. Michael's not home yet / not here. Can I take a message?

D With your partner, play one of these roles in a phone conversation. Use the Useful Expressions to help you.

Student A: You call your friend to invite him or her to a movie. Your friend isn't home. Leave a message with a family member.

Student B: Answer the phone. Take a message. Fill out the note on the right.

While You Were Out

Time of Call: ______________

Name of Caller: ______________

Message: ______________

____

E Switch roles and practice again.

5 GRAMMAR

A Turn to page 236. Complete the exercise. Then do **B–D** below.

The Present Continuous as Future			
Subject + *be*	**Verb + *ing***		**Future time expressions**
We're	seeing	a movie	today / tonight / tomorrow. in an hour. this weekend.
They're	making		next year.

B Complete the time expressions with a word from the box. One item does not need a word.

in	the	this / next

1. ________ day after tomorrow
2. ________ month
3. ________ tonight
4. ________ a few days

C Work with a partner. Four of the sentences below correctly use the present continuous tense to talk about future plans, but two sentences do not. Cross out the two incorrect sentences.

1. We're seeing a movie later today.
2. I'm meeting them in front of the theater at 2:00.
3. We're having a lot of snow next week.
4. They're watching the Oscars tonight.
5. You need to rest or you're getting sick.
6. We're going out of town this weekend.

Events that you can plan: a vacation, meeting friends on the weekend
Events that you cannot plan: the weather, illness
Do not use the present continuous as future for events that you cannot plan.

D Look at the sentences you didn't cross out in **C**. Work with a partner to make a short conversation using at least three of the sentences.

People lining up outside of the Oscars

WORLD LINK

The Oscars are a movie awards show in the US. Go online to find out which movie won "Best Picture" last year. What country was the "Best Foreign Film" from?

6 COMMUNICATION

A Work in a small group. You are going to create a poster for a new movie. Follow the steps below.

1. Write the names of two people in your movie.

   famous actor: ____________________ famous actress: ____________________

2. Choose one of the following to appear in your movie.

   a monster a superhero a cowboy

   an alien a spy your idea: ____________________

3. Choose a location for your movie: ____________________

4. What kind of movie is it? Circle one.

   action movie horror film sci-fi thriller

   drama romantic comedy other: ____________________

5. Finally, choose a title for your movie: ____________________

B Now make the poster advertising your movie. Put your group's poster on the wall.

C Walk around and look at all the posters. Which movie do you want to see? Invite two people to see the movie with you.

The Monster Next Door looks really good.

It does. I'm a big fan of scary movies. They make me scream!

Me too. Hey, I'm seeing it tonight at 7:00. Do you want to come?

Sorry, but I can't. I'm going to a different movie then.

LESSON B MOVIE REVIEWS

A scene from a Bollywood film

1 VOCABULARY

A The people below watched different movies recently.

1. Take turns with a partner. Read each opinion aloud.
2. Did the person like the movie? Why or why not?

Word Bank

Word Partnerships

You can **go to** / **see** / **watch** a movie.

I watched *The Hunger Games*. It was very **suspenseful**. I kept thinking, "What's going to happen next?"

I watched a Bollywood movie. It was really **entertaining**. There was a lot of singing and dancing, and it was a **sweet** love story, too. It was a lot of fun.

You need to see *Invictus*. It's about a rugby team from South Africa. It's very **inspiring**. You feel good and you think about life, too.

I saw a **depressing** movie last weekend. It was so sad that I stopped watching it.

I saw a **hilarious** movie last night. The comic in it was really funny.

I watched this **scary** zombie movie with my boyfriend. He's crazy about them, but for me, they're too **violent**. There's too much blood!

B Now think of movies you know. Tell your partner your ideas.

Name a(n) __________ movie.

1. suspenseful
2. hilarious
3. inspiring
4. depressing
5. entertaining
6. sweet
7. scary
8. violent

2 LISTENING

A Read the definitions in the Word Bank. Then answer the questions. Tell a partner.

1. Where do you usually see movie trailers?

   online   on TV   at the movies

2. What movie is coming out soon? Name one.

> A new *Star Wars* movie is coming out this year.

Word Bank

A *movie trailer* is an ad. It shows some scenes from a movie.

When a movie *comes out*, it is available to watch.

B **Listen for a speaker's opinion.** A man and woman are talking about movies. Listen and circle the correct opinion (1a–6a) below. **Track 77**

Opinion	Reason
1a. The woman likes / dislikes the *Fast Cars* movies.	1b. They are good stories / violent.
2a. The man likes / dislikes the *Fast Cars* movies.	2b. They are entertaining / hilarious.
3a. The woman likes / dislikes actress Laura Swift.	3b. She is / isn't funny.
4a. The man likes / dislikes Laura Swift.	4b. She is / isn't funny.
5a. The woman wants / doesn't want to see Laura Swift's new movie.	5b. Her new movie sounds sad / hilarious.
6a. The man wants / doesn't want to see Laura Swift's new movie.	6b. Her new movie is funny / inspiring.

C **Listen for details.** What reason does each person give? Listen again and circle the correct reason (1b–6b) in **B**. **Track 77**

D **Listen for details.** Listen again. Circle T for *true* and F for *false*. If a sentence is false, make it true. **Track 77**

1. *Fast Cars 4* is an action movie.	T	F
2. *Fast Cars 4* is coming out next week.	T	F
3. Laura Swift's new movie is a comedy.	T	F
4. In her new movie, Laura Swift is a rich woman in London.	T	F

E With a partner, take turns asking the questions about the two movies you heard about.

1. What kind of movie is it?
2. Do you like these kinds of movies? Why or why not?

> What kind of movie is Fast Cars 4?

3 READING

A **Use background knowledge.** Look at the reading. One movie is the original; the other is a *remake* (a new version of an old film). Do you know any movie remakes?

B **Make predictions.** Look at the photos. Guess the answer to the question.

What words describe the movie *Shutter*?

a. hilarious c. inspiring

b. scary d. suspenseful

C **Check predictions.** Read the movie descriptions. Check your answer(s) in **B**.

What information in the reading helped you confirm or change your answer(s)? Underline it.

D **Read for details.** Which movie does each sentence describe? Check *original*, *remake*, or both.

1. The man's name is Tun.
   ☐ original ☐ remake
2. The man is a photographer.
   ☐ original ☐ remake
3. There is a car accident.
   ☐ original ☐ remake
4. They see a girl in the photos.
   ☐ original ☐ remake
5. The story takes place in Japan.
   ☐ original ☐ remake
6. The critics didn't like this movie.
   ☐ original ☐ remake

E Answer the questions with a partner.

1. Would you like to see this movie—either the original or the remake? Why or why not?
2. What movies should not be remade?

A MOVIE REMAKE

Track 78

SHUTTER (original)

In this popular film from Thailand, Tun, a photographer, and his girlfriend, Jane, are driving home on a lonely country road one night. Suddenly they see a girl in the road. Jane tries to stop the car, but it's too late. She hits and kills the girl. Feeling very afraid, Tun and Jane leave the girl and quickly drive back home to Bangkok.

Jane and Tun try to return to normal life, but then strange things start happening. Tun starts to have bad neck pain. And both Jane and Tun see strange images in Tun's photographs. They look like a girl. Is it the girl on the road?

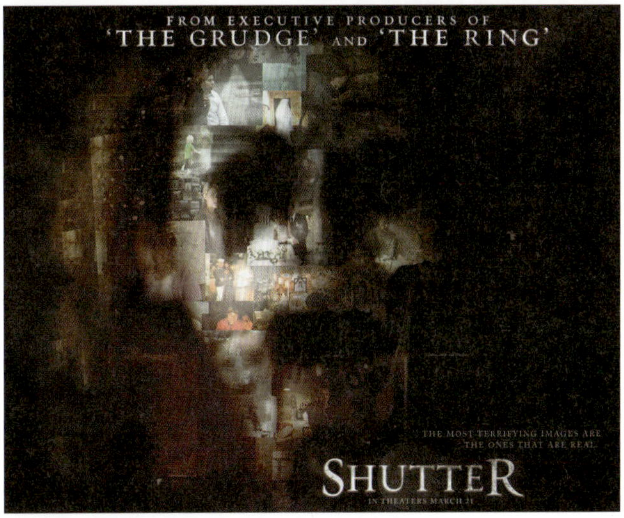

SHUTTER (remake)

This movie is an American remake of a Thai movie with the same name. The critics[1] thought the film would flop,[2] but it did well and made over $45 million worldwide.

The main characters are Jane and her husband Ben. They move to Tokyo for Ben's new job as a photographer. One night they are in a car accident on a country road. They hit a young girl and drive into a tree. When they wake up, they look for the girl, but they can't find her. Was the girl really there?

Jane and Ben try to forget the frightening experience, but they can't. Then Ben's shoulder starts to hurt all the time. And when Ben looks at his photos, there are strange lights in them. Ben's helper, Seiko, thinks the lights look like a girl. Is it the girl on the road?

[1]A movie *critic* watches movies and gives an opinion about them.
[2]If a movie *flops*, it isn't successful.

4 GRAMMAR

A Turn to page 237. Complete the exercises. Then do **B–D** below.

-ed Adjectives	*-ing* Adjectives
I'm **bored**. I don't like this movie.	This movie is **boring**. Let's watch something else.

B Read the conversation. Complete each sentence with the correct adjective. Then work in a group of three and practice the conversation.

A: What did you do this weekend?

B: Not much. Mostly I watched movies.

C: What did you see?

A: I saw *Midnight on the Moon*. It was good. I was surprised / surprising.

B: Really? I saw that movie, too. I was kind of bored / boring by it.

A: You're kidding. It was amazed / amazing.

B: In my opinion, it was kind of slow and depressed / depressing in places.

A: Did you see the movie, Juan?

C: Yeah, I did.

A: What did you think?

C: Well, parts of the movie were bored / boring, but mostly it was entertained / entertaining. And the ending was excited / exciting.

A: I thought so, too!

C In the same group, think of a movie you all saw. Then, on your own, use *-ed* / *-ing* adjectives to give your opinion of the movie.

A movie we all saw: ______________________

My opinion of the movie: ______________________

How I felt watching it (use an *-ed* adjective): ______________________

How the movie was (use an *-ing* adjective): ______________________

D Use the conversation in **B** and your ideas in **C** to talk about your movie.

5 WRITING

A Read about one person's favorite movie. Answer the questions with a partner.

1. What is the writer's favorite movie?
2. What kind of movie is it? What is it about?
3. What happens in the movie?

My Favorite Movie

My favorite movie of all time is *Cinema Paradiso*. It's a classic film from the 1980s. It's about an Italian boy named Salvatore. He loves movies.

In the film, Salvatore remembers his childhood. When he was young, he watched movies at the Cinema Paradiso, a theater in his hometown. He had an old friend named Alfredo, and he loved a girl named Elena. The movie is about these people's lives. It is a very sweet and inspiring film. You should see it!

Cinema Paradiso is *set* in Palazzo Adriano, Italy. Where a movie is set is where it takes place.

B Answer the questions in **A** about your favorite movie. Write your ideas in a few words.

C Write two paragraphs about your movie. Use your notes in **B**.

- Paragraph 1: Say the name of the movie, the kind of movie it is, and what it's about.
- Paragraph 2: Explain what happens in the movie.
- In your writing, use adjectives from this lesson.
- End with a short sentence. Tell people to see the movie.

D Exchange papers with a partner.

1. Answer the questions in **A** about your partner's movie.
2. Circle mistakes in your partner's writing. Then return the paper to him or her.

E Make corrections to your writing. Then put together a "Must-See Movies" list with all of your classmates' ideas.

6 COMMUNICATION

A Prepare a short talk about your favorite movie.

1. Practice: Use your notes from Writing to talk about it.
2. Find a short movie trailer to use in your presentation.

B Work in a group of four. Give your presentation.

When you listen, take notes. Answer the questions in Writing **A** about your partners' movies.

C Your group talked about four movies. What do you think of each one?

Use the sentences below to tell your group.

I saw ______________,...
☐ and I liked it because...
☐ but I didn't like it because...

I did not see ______________,...
☐ but now I'd like to see it.
☐ and I don't plan to see it.

I saw *Thor*, but I didn't like it. I'm not into movies about comic book characters.

MEMO

NATIONAL GEOGRAPHIC LEARNING

MEMO

KEIMYUNG UNIVERSITY

1 LISTENING

A Look at the pictures. Do these things ever happen where you live? Tell a partner.

☐ how to survive a tornado

☐ how to survive a house fire

☐ how to survive an earthquake

B Listen. Tom is talking to a group of students. What are they talking about? Check (✓) the correct answer above. **Track 79**

C What rules do you think Tom is going to say? Make predictions. Then listen to the full conversation. Check (✓) the correct answers. **Track 80**

☐ Open the windows.
☐ Get under a desk.
☐ Go to the store for food and water.
☐ Don't stand near the windows.
☐ Go outdoors and stand in the street.
☐ Don't use matches.

2 JOB ADS

A Look at the job ads. Can you do these jobs? Tell your partner.

> I can do the receptionist job.
> I can type quickly and...

Sundance Studio needs an outgoing dance teacher!

Teach children to dance

You: Friendly and outgoing dance teacher.
Work well with children ages 6-8.

Days and hours: Thursday, Friday, and Saturday part-time, 5-9 PM.

Pay: $35 per hour

Wanted: Friendly, hardworking receptionist for an international office

You: Type quickly
Speak English on the phone
It helps if you can speak one of these languages: Chinese, Japanese, Korean, Portuguese, Russian, Spanish, or Thai.

Days and hours: Monday – Friday 8 AM – 5 PM.

Pay: $28,000 per year

B Now make your own job ad on a piece of paper. Write the name of the job, the responsibilities and requirements, the days and hours, and the pay.

C Put your ad on the classroom wall. Read the other ads. Which jobs can you do? Make a list.

D Tell a partner about the jobs on your list. Which jobs are good for you? Why?

3 WHAT DO YOU DO?

A **Predict.** Look at the photos. Can you guess any information in the chart? Work with a partner.

Name	Job	Where	What's the job like?	Wants to...
Bill	____________	at a place called The Matrix	works ____________	have his own restaurant
Kira	works for herself	has a ____________ store online	great, but she's ____________ busy	get someone to ____________ her
Juan	____________	in ____________	sometimes ____________	work during the ____________
Diya	is doing an internship as a ____________	at a tech company	interesting	get a ____________ job there

B **Listen for details.** Listen. Complete the chart above with the correct word(s). **Track 81**

C Answer the questions. Then ask a partner four *Wh-* questions of your own about the people.

1. What does Bill do?
2. Where does Juan work?
3. Who works for herself?
4. What is Juan's job like?
5. Who works a lot?
6. In the future, what does Diya want to do?

D Work with a partner. Make a dialog between two people in the photos. Use the notes in the chart and your own ideas. Try to talk for two minutes.

So, what do you do, Bill?

I'm a chef.

What's that like?

It's interesting, but I have to work a lot.

4 SEE IT AND SAY IT

A Talk about the picture with a partner.

- What's happening in the scene?
- Who looks surprised? bored? excited?
- What kind of movie is it?

B Get into a group of three or four people. You are going to perform the movie scene in the picture.

1. Discuss the scene. What's happening? Why do you think it's happening?
2. Choose a person in the scene to role-play.
3. Create a short role play of six to eight sentences. Practice it with your group.

C Perform your scene for the class.

UNIT 1 PEOPLE

LESSON A

Vocabulary

born in
city
contact information
email address
favorites
first / **last name**
friends
hometown
interested in
job
languages
phone number
subject

Speaking Strategy

Introducing Yourself

A: My name is Mariana.
B: Hi, I'm Danny. (It's) Nice to meet you.
A: (It's) Nice to meet you, too.

Asking about Occupations

A: What do you do?
B: I'm a music student.

LESSON B

Vocabulary

Use *be* with…

Age
young
in his / **her teens***
in his / **her twenties***
elderly (80+)

Weight
skinny
thin
slim**
average weight
heavy

Height
short
average
tall

Use *have* with…

Eye color
(**dark**) **brown**
blue
green

Hairstyle
long ↔ **short**
straight ↔ **curly**
wavy
spiky

Hair color
black
(**light** / **dark**) **brown**
blond
red
gray

Facial hair
beard
mustache

*teens (13–19), twenties (ages 20–29), thirties, forties, etc.
***Slim* means *skinny* / *thin*, but *slim* has a positive meaning.

UNIT 2 ACTIVITIES

LESSON A

Vocabulary

do (homework)
dorm
drink (soda)
eat (pizza)
exercise
go (to school)
have a great time
improve
listen (to music)
roommate
shop
study (for a test)
talk (on the phone)
term
text (a friend)
watch TV

Speaking Strategy

Greeting people and asking how they are

Positive response
A: Hi, (Sara). How are you doing?
B: Fine. / OK. / All right. / Not bad. How about you?
A: I'm fine, thanks.

Negative response
A: Hi, (Yuki). How's it going?
B: So-so. / Not so good.
A: Really? / Yeah? What's wrong?
B: I'm waiting for the bus. It's late!

LESSON B

Vocabulary

School subjects and college majors*
art
business
engineering
graphic design
history
information technology (IT)
law
math
nursing
science
tourism / hospitality

*A ***school subject*** is an area of study. Your ***major*** is your main subject of study in college.

Talking about your studies
Where do you go to school?
I go to / I'm a student at the Fashion Institute of Technology.

What are you studying?
I'm studying music / medicine.
I'm majoring in business.
I'm preparing for the college entrance exam.

What classes are you taking?
I'm taking a test-prep **class.** /
I'm taking two business **classes.**

UNIT 3 SHOPPING

LESSON A

Vocabulary

apple
(a bunch of) **bananas**
(ground) **beef**
(a loaf of) **bread**
butter
(a piece of) **cake**
(a bunch of) **carrots**
(a box of) **cereal**
cheese
chicken
coffee
chips
(a carton of) **eggs**
fish
(a bunch of) **grapes**
(a carton of) **ice cream**
(a head of) **lettuce**
milk
noodles
(orange) **juice**
rice
salad
(a can of) **soda**
soup
sugar
tea
tofu
tomato
yogurt

fresh / frozen / junk **food**

Speaking Strategy

Talking about things you need
Do we need anything?
Yes, we do. We need soda and bottled water.
Let's see… we need…
No, we don't. We (already) have everything.
What else do we need?
We still need…
Nothing. I think we're all set.
Anything else?
Yes, we need…
No, that's it. We have everything.

LESSON B

Vocabulary

affordable ↔ **expensive**
buy ↔ **sell**
cash
credit card
debit card
full price
go shopping
mall
on sale
pay
shop (*for* something / *at* a place)
shop / **spend** (**money**)

UNIT 4 VACATION

LESSON A

Vocabulary

clear
cloudy
foggy
rainy
snowy
sunny
windy

raining
snowing

(**partly** / **mostly**) (**cloudy** / **sunny**)
high / **low** (**temperature**)

chilly
cold
comfortable
freezing
hot
warm

30° = thirty degrees
–5° = minus five degrees

Speaking Strategy

Giving Advice

(I think) you should take a sweater.
  Good idea. / OK, I will.
  Really? I don't think so. /
  Really? I'd rather not.
I don't think you should drive. /
You shouldn't drive.
  You're probably right.
  Really? I think I'll be OK.

LESSON B

Vocabulary

buy a plane ticket
check in to ↔ check out of (a hotel)
get a passport
go on vacation / go on a trip
go sightseeing
pack ↔ **unpack** (a suitcase)
post photos online
take photos

UNIT 5 FOOD

LESSON A

Vocabulary

beans
bread
cheese
coffee
(fried) chicken
eggs
fish
fruit
(orange) juice
meat
milk
onions
pasta
(baked) potato
rice
(spinach) salad
(tuna) sandwich
soda
(vegetable) soup
spaghetti
steak
tea
tomato (sauce)
vegetable

breakfast
lunch
dinner

hungry
meal

Speaking Strategy

Talking about likes and dislikes
Do you like (Indian) food?
Do you like (fish)?

Yes! I love it!
Yes, I like it a lot.
Yeah, it's OK.
No, not really.
No, I can't stand it.

LESSON B

Vocabulary

bananas
cancer
(a) cold
energy
good for you ↔ **bad for you**
have / eat breakfast
healthy ↔ **unhealthy**
high (in) ↔ **low (in) (calories / sugar / protein)**
honey
ice
ice cream
illness
junk food
medicine
milk
oranges
skin
skip (breakfast)
snack
stomach
strawberries
taste good ↔ **taste bad**
vitamins
yogurt

UNIT 6 RELATIONSHIPS

LESSON A

Vocabulary

grandparents
grandmother
grandfather

parents
mother
father

(older) sister
(younger) brother

aunt
uncle
cousin

wife
husband
daughter
son
baby
children

Speaking Strategy

Asking and answering questions about family

How many people are (there) in your family?
(There are) four: me, my brother, and my parents.

Do you have any brothers and sisters?
Yes, I have a sister. / No, I'm an only child.

Are you close (to your sister)?
Yes, I am. / No, not really.

LESSON B

Vocabulary

boyfriend
(be) dating / seeing someone
girlfriend
ex-husband / wife
(be) married
(be) single

Talking about relationships
marriage (n)
marry, get married (v)
(be) married (adj)

divorce (n)
divorce, get divorced (v)
(be) divorced (adj)

Talking about age
How old are you?
I'm... (years old).

10 ten	24 twenty-four
11 eleven	25 twenty-five
12 twelve	26 twenty-six
13 thirteen	27 twenty-seven
14 fourteen	28 twenty-eight
15 fifteen	29 twenty-nine
16 sixteen	30 thirty
17 seventeen	40 forty
18 eighteen	50 fifty
19 nineteen	60 sixty
20 twenty	70 seventy
21 twenty-one	80 eighty
22 twenty-two	90 ninety
23 twenty-three	100 one hundred

UNIT 7 TIME

LESSON A

Vocabulary

wake up
take a shower
get dressed
leave home
start (class)
finish (class)
study
go home
do homework
go to bed

two (o'clock)
two-oh-five / five after two
two fifteen / quarter after two
two thirty / half past two
two forty-five / quarter to three
two fifty-five / five to three

in the morning / afternoon / evening
at noon / midnight
at night

yesterday / today / tonight / tomorrow

early / late

Speaking Strategy

Making suggestions
Let's see a movie.
We could see a movie.

Saying *yes*
(That) sounds good.
Good / Great idea.

Saying *no* politely
I don't really like French food.
I don't really want to see that movie.

LESSON B

Vocabulary

(a) day off
go dancing, shopping
go for a walk, bike ride, run
go out with friends, family, your boyfriend or girlfriend
go to the movies, gym, beach, a club, concert, party, friend's house
(on) the weekend
spend time with (someone)

UNIT 8 CITY LIFE

LESSON A

Vocabulary

ATM / **cash machine**
bookstore
bus station
coffee shop / **cafe**
copy shop
department store
gas station
grocery store / **supermarket**
hair salon
health club / **gym**
nail salon
newsstand / **kiosk**
nightclub
police station
taxi stand
train station

neighborhood

Speaking Strategy

Asking for and giving directions
Asking about a place in general:
Excuse me. Is there a (gas station) near here?
Yes. Go one block. There's one on the corner of (Court Street and First Avenue).

Asking about a specific place:
Excuse me. Where's the (Bridge Theater)?
It's on (Jay Street).
Go straight and turn right (on Jay Street).
It's in the middle of the block.

LESSON B

Vocabulary

a lot of ↔ a little **pollution** (*n.*)
very ↔ not very **polluted** (*adj.*)
heavy ↔ light **traffic**
stuck in traffic
population
(public) transportation
rush hour

UNIT 9 ALL ABOUT YOU

LESSON A

Vocabulary

play...
badminton
baseball
basketball
hockey
ping pong
soccer
tennis
volleyball

cards
darts
golf
rugby

do...
judo
pilates
yoga

gymnastics
crafts
kickboxing
puzzles

go...
bowling
jogging
skiing
surfing
swimming

camping
climbing
fishing
golfing

Speaking Strategy

Inviting with *Do you want*
Do you want to come?
[*want* + *to* + verb]
Sure, I'd love to!
Sorry, I can't. I'm busy.
Um, no thanks. I'm not good at…

Offering with *Do you want*
Do you want some ice cream?
[*want* + noun]
Yes, please. / Yes, thanks.
No, thank you. / No, thanks. I'm fine.

LESSON B

Vocabulary

ambitious ↔ **laid-back** / relaxed
bright / intelligent
careful ↔ **careless**
competitive
creative
generous ↔ **selfish**
impulsive ↔ **careful**
organized ↔ **messy**
patient ↔ impatient
private
shy
talkative ↔ **reserved**
workaholic

UNIT 10 HEALTH

LESSON A

Vocabulary

arm
back
chest
foot
hand
head
- **ear**
- **eye**
- **face**
- **nose**
- **mouth**

leg
neck
shoulder
stomach

broad ↔ **narrow** shoulders
long ↔ **short** arms / legs
big / **large** ↔ **little** / **small** (eyes / nose)
muscular (body)

backache
skin
fever
headache
sore throat
stomachache
temperature

Speaking Strategy

Talking about health problems
What's wrong? / What's the matter?
- I don't feel well.
- I'm sick.
- I have a / an (fever)
- My (leg) hurts

LESSON B

Vocabulary

be full of ↔ **be low on** (**energy**)

deal with (stress / a problem)
have time (to do something)
make a schedule

reduce (stress)
stressed ↔ relaxed
stressful ↔ relaxing
take time (to do something)

be under pressure
take a break
wait until the last minute

UNIT 11 JOBS

LESSON A

Vocabulary

businessperson
cashier
chef
delivery person
doctor
flight attendant
hairstylist
lawyer
nurse
police officer
programmer
receptionist
reporter
telemarketer
tutor
waiter / waitress
web designer

business card

Speaking Strategy

Talking about jobs
What do you do?
What does he / she do?

I'm a student / programmer / doctor.
He's a waiter. / She's a nurse.
I work for Telefonica / Bank of China / DHL Global Mail / myself.
She works in a hospital / an office / a cafe.

LESSON B

Vocabulary

do an internship
(have, get) experience
(have a) full-time ↔ part-time job
(work) full time ↔ part time
get a job
goal
make money
pay

Using large numbers / Talking about pay

I want to make... (dollars) a (year).

1,000	one thousand
2,000	two thousand
10,000	ten thousand
50,000	fifty thousand
100,000	one hundred thousand
150,000	one hundred fifty thousand
500,000	five hundred thousand / half a million
1,000,000	one million
1,000,000,000	one billion

UNIT 12 AT THE MOVIES

LESSON A

Vocabulary

action movie
blockbuster
chick flick
classic / **old movie**
documentary
drama
horror film
indie
musical
romantic comedy
science fiction (**sci-fi**) **thriller**
tearjerker

make you (laugh / cry / think / scream)

(not) a (big) fan of (something)
(not) crazy about (something)
(not) into (something)

Speaking Strategy

Taking and leaving a message

Hello? Is Michael there?
Who's calling, please?
This is Silvio.
OK. Hang on a minute.
Sorry. Michael's not home yet / not here. Can I take a message?

LESSON B

Vocabulary

depressing
entertaining
hilarious
inspiring
scary
suspenseful
sweet
violent
go / **see** / **watch** a movie

UNIT 1 PEOPLE

LESSON A

The Simple Present Tense						
Affirmative statements			**Negative statements**			
I / You / We / They	speak	English.	I / You / We / They	don't	speak	English.
He / She / It	speaks		He / She / It	doesn't		

Yes / No* questions with *be				**Short answers**	
Is	she	a	student?	Yes, she **is**.	No, she**'s** not.* / No, she **is**n't.
Are	you			Yes, I **am**.	No, I**'m** not.
	they		students?	Yes, they **are**.	No, they**'re** not.* / No, they **are**n't.

*In spoken English, this negative form is more common.

***Yes / No* questions with other verbs**				**Short answers**	
Do	you	**speak**	English?	Yes, I **do**.	No, I **don't**.
Does	she			Yes, she **does**.	No, she **doesn't**.

***Wh-* questions**				**Short answers**
Where	do	you	live?	I live in Buenos Aires.
	does	he		He still lives in his hometown.
What	do	you	do?	I'm a student.
	does	she		She's a doctor.

A Complete the questions and answers. Then match each question to an appropriate answer.

1. ______ you live alone?
2. ______ ______ you do for fun?
3. ______ you a good student?
4. ______ ______ you live with?
5. ______ you a teacher?
6. ______ is your part-time job?

a. No, ______ ______. I'm a student.
b. My mother and father.
c. Yes, ______ ______. I get good grades.
d. I'm in a band.
e. I'm an office clerk.
f. No, I ______. I live with my family.

LESSON B

Describing Appearance			
Subject	***be / have***	**Adjective**	**Noun**
He	**is**	tall.	
		average	height / weight.
		young / in his teens.	
	has	blue	eyes.
		short, black	hair.

Use *be* to describe a person's height, weight, and age.

Use *have* to describe a person's eye color, hairstyle and color, and facial hair.

*The exceptions: He **is** bald. (He has no hair on his head.)
He **is** clean-shaven. (He has no hair on his face.)

When using two or more adjectives, the words usually follow this pattern:
length / size—style—color

He has **short, curly, red** hair.   She has **big blue** eyes.

A Complete the sentences with the correct form of *be* or *have*.

1. Tanya's dad ______ average height.
2. Ricardo and his sister ______ wavy hair.
3. My grandmother ______ in her eighties. She ______ elderly.
4. I ______ green eyes.
5. Max and Charlie are brothers. Max ______ a beard and mustache. Charlie ______ clean-shaven. They both ______ blond hair.
6. Damon ______ heavy. He weighs 150 kilos.

B Look at the photo and make sentences about the woman. Describe her appearance.

Name: Lupita Nyong'o

Job: Actress

Nationality: Kenyan, Mexican

Hair: She ____________________ hair.

Eyes: She ____________________ eyes.

Age: She ____________________ in her ____________________.

Weight: She ____________________.

C Tell a partner about the woman in **B**.

UNIT 2 ACTIVITIES

LESSON A

The Present Continuous Tense: Affirmative and Negative Statements				
Subject pronoun	***be***	***(not)***	**verb + *-ing***	**Contractions with *be***
I	**am**	(not)	**working.**	I am = I'm; I am not = I'm not
You	**are**			you are = you're; you are not = you're not / you aren't
He / She / It	**is**			she is = she's; she is not = she's not / she isn't
We / They	**are**			we are = we're; we are not = we're not / we aren't

The Present Continuous Tense: *Wh-* Questions and Answers and *Yes / No* Questions and Answers				
Question word	***be***	**subject**	**verb + *-ing***	**Answers**
What	**are**	you	**doing?**	(I'm) **exercising.**
	is	he		(He's) **exercising.**
	are	they		(They're) **exercising.**
Where	**are**	you	**sitting?**	(We're) **sitting** in the front.
	be	**subject**	**verb + *-ing***	**Short answers**
	Are	you	**studying?**	Yes, I am. No, I'm not. I'm **texting.**
	Is	she		Yes, she is. No, she's not. / No, she isn't. She's **reading.**
	Are	you		Yes, we are. No, we're not. / No, we aren't. We're **swimming.**
		they		Yes, they are. No, they aren't. / No, they're not. They're **working.**

Spelling rules for verb + *ing*

In most cases, add *ing* to the base form of the verb: *work* → *work**ing***

If the verb ends in an *e*, drop the *e* and add *ing*: *exercise* → *exercis**ing***

If the verb has one syllable and ends in a consonant + vowel + consonant, double the final consonant and add *ing*: *sit* → *sit**ting*** (This does not apply if the verb ends in *w, x,* or *y*: *row* → *row**ing***.)

A Complete the sentences with the appropriate words. Use contractions where possible.

1. A: ___Are___ you (take) ___taking___ the bus?
   B: No, ____________. I (walk) ____________.
2. A: What ____________ they (do) ____________ at the gym?
   B: They ____________ (run) ____________ and (swim) ____________.
3. A: ____________ you (use) ____________ this computer?
   B: No, we ____________. We (talk) ____________.

4. A: Where ______ she (study) ______?
   B: At the English lab. She (listen) ______ to questions and (write) ______ the answers.

5. A: ______ he still (sleep) ______?
   B: No, he ______. He ______ already (work) ______.

LESSON B

The Present Continuous Tense: Extended Time	
A: What **are** you **doing** right now? B: I'**m studying** for a test at the moment.	You can use the present continuous to talk about actions happening now, at the moment of speaking. Notice the time expressions.
A: What **are** you **doing** these days / nowadays? B: I'**m studying** in Hong Kong this term. A: **Are** you **enjoying** Hong Kong? B: Yes, I'**m having** a great time!	You can also use the present continuous to talk about actions continuing for a period of time in the present. Notice the time expressions.

A Monika is traveling in Ecuador for a month. Read her email to a friend. Complete the sentences with the present continuous tense.

Hi Kira,

(1. I / write) ______ to you from Ecuador. Today, (2. our group / visit) ______ Quito, the capital city. It's really beautiful. Right now, (3. we / eat) ______ lunch. The food here is so good!

(4. I / enjoy) ______ this program. This week, (5. we / learn) ______ about the rainforest and the animals in Ecuador. (6. I / also / use) ______ my Spanish a lot, and that's great. There's only one bad thing: (7. it / rain) ______ a lot these days. But (8. the rain / not / stop) ______ us. We are outside every day.

Well, (9. we / leave) ______ the cafe now, so that's all my news for today. (10. you / do) ______ anything fun this month?

Write soon,

Monika

B Answer the questions. Write the numbers (1–10) from **A** on the correct line.

Which sentences in **A** are about…

1. actions happening right now? ______________________
2. actions continuing for a period of time in the present? ______________________

UNIT 3 SHOPPING

LESSON A

Count Nouns		Noncount Nouns		
Singular	**Plural**			
apple carrot tomato	apples carrots tomatoes	beef cereal rice	bread cheese soda	English divides nouns into things we can count (count nouns) and things we can't (noncount nouns). Count nouns have singular and plural forms.

Singular and Plural Count Nouns; Noncount Nouns					
	Article	**Noun**	**Verb**		
Singular count nouns	A	banana	is	a good snack.	Use *a* / *an* or *the* before the noun.
	The	banana	is	in the bowl.	Use a singular form of the verb.
Plural count nouns	—	Bananas	are	good for you.	Use *the* or no article before the noun.
	The	bananas	are	on the table.	Use a plural form of the verb.
Noncount nouns	—	Bread	is	inexpensive.	Use *the* or no article before the noun.
	The	bread	is	in the bag.	Use a singular form of the verb.

Partitives: Talking about Specific Amounts							
General amount			**Specific amount**				
Please buy	some	bread.	Please buy	a	loaf	of	bread.
		lettuce.			head		lettuce.
		ice cream.			carton		eggs.
		carrots.			bunch		grapes.

a bottle of water a can of soup / soda	a glass of juice / water a piece of cake / chocolate	a cup of coffee / soup a slice of bread / pie

A Read this recipe for beef stir fry. Circle the count nouns. Underline the noncount ones.

Pour some (1.) oil into (2.) a pan and heat it up.

Add (3.) some garlic, (4.) mushrooms, and (5.) carrots into the pan and cook them.

Remove the garlic and (6.) the vegetables from the pan.

Next, cook (7.) the beef.

Put (8.) the meat and (9.) vegetables together and cover with (10.) soy sauce.

Serve over (11.) rice on (12.) a dinner plate.

Don't forget to have (13.) a drink with it!

LESSON B

	Yes / No Questions with *any*		Answers
Plural count nouns	Do you have **any**	friends?	Yes, I do.
Noncount nouns		money?	No, I don't.

Use *any* in *Yes / No* questions to ask about unknown amounts.

Quantifiers with Affirmative and Negative Statements			
		Quantifier	Noun
Plural count nouns	I have	**a lot of / many** **some**	friends.
	I don't have	**a lot of / many** **any**	
Noncount nouns	I have	**a lot of** **some**	money.
	I don't have	**a lot of / much** **any**	

Quantifiers give information about an amount of something.
You can answer a question with a short answer:

*Do you have **any** friends?* — *Yes, I have **a lot** (**of** friends).*

*Do you have **any** money?* — *No, I don't have **much** (money), just two dollars.*

Notice: *I don't have **any** friends / money.* = *I have **no** friends / money.*

A Complete each sentence with the best answer.

1. Juan has $1,000,000. He has much / a lot of money.
2. Barry only has $2. He doesn't have any / much money.
3. This store only sells clothes. You can't buy any / many shoes here.
4. Rita has a lot of / many beautiful jewelry.
5. There aren't much / many department stores in this city. There are only two.
6. Leo has three friends. He has many / some friends.

B Write a quantifier in each blank. Then practice the dialogs with a partner.

1. A: Do you have ______________ questions about the homework?
   B: No, I don't have ______________. I understand everything.
2. A: Are there ______________ girls in this class?
   B: Yes, there are ______________—three, I think.
3. A: Do you have ______________ cash? I want a soda.
   B: Yes, but I don't have ______________. I only have $1.
4. A: Is there ______________ room in the closet for my suitcase?
   B: Yes, the closet is empty. There's ______________ room.

UNIT 4 VACATION

LESSON A

Connecting Ideas with *but, or,* and *so*	
It's freezing in Moscow, **but** it's warm in Rio. It's cold **but** sunny in Lima today. It's a nice day **but** a little hot.	Use *but* to show an opposite idea or contrast. *But* joins words, phrases, and sentences.
We can go to the beach, **or** we can visit the zoo. Is it warm **or** chilly outside? Do you want coffee **or** tea?	Use *or* to give choices. *Or* joins words, phrases, and sentences.
It's raining, **so** we're not having a picnic today. My hometown is Seoul, **so** I know it well.	Use *so* to introduce a result. *So* joins sentences.

A Complete the sentences with *but, or,* or *so*.

1. William can't speak French, _______ Marion can.
2. Roberto is very healthy. He doesn't drink _______ smoke.
3. It's foggy outside, _______ I don't think you need sunglasses.
4. Does the movie start at 7:00 _______ 7:30?
5. Tokyo is an exciting city, _______ it's very expensive to live in.
6. It's 32° C / 90° F out, _______ I'm wearing a T-shirt.
7. It's snowing outside, _______ Mario is wearing shorts.
8. For dinner, you can have chicken, fish, _______ beef.

B Combine the two sentences using *but, or,* or *so*.

1. Kaz likes to travel. His girlfriend doesn't like to travel.
   Kaz likes to travel, but his girlfriend doesn't_______________.
2. We can go to Martin's party. We can see a movie.
   ____.
3. John is sick. He's not coming to class today.
   ____.
4. It's a beautiful day. We're having class outside.
   ____.
5. I'm wearing my glasses. I can't see the whiteboard.
   ____.
6. Rosa wants to study at an American university. She's taking the TOEFL exam.
   ____.

LESSON B

	Possessive Adjectives	Possessive Pronouns	*belong to*
Whose passport is this?	It's **my** passport.	It's **mine.**	It **belongs to me.**
	your	**yours.**	**you.**
	her	**hers.**	**her.**
	his	**his.**	**him.**
	our	**ours.**	**us.**
	their	**theirs.**	**them.**

Whose and *who's* have the same pronunciation but different meanings.
Whose asks about the owner of something: *Whose house is that? It's mine.*
Who's is a contraction of *Who* and *is*: *Who's studying English? Maria is.*

A Write the correct possessive pronoun for the underlined words.

1. A: That's not her suitcase.
   B: No, her suitcase (hers) is over there.
2. A: Can I use your cell phone? My cell phone doesn't work.
   B: Sorry, but I forgot my cell phone at home. Use Jon's phone.
3. A: Is your class fun?
   B: Yes, but Aya and Leo's class is more interesting.
4. A: Is your hometown hot in the summer? My hometown is.
   B: Our hometown is, too.
5. A: Your birthday is in May.
   B: That's right, and your birthday is in March.

B Use the words in the chart to complete the conversation. Then practice the dialog with a partner.

JIM: Well, I have (1.) ___my___ luggage. Where's (2.) __________?

BEN: Um... let's see... oh, here's (3.) __________ suitcase. No, wait... this one isn't (4.) __________.

JIM: (5.) __________ is it?

BEN: It says Mr. Simon Konig. It belongs to (6.) __________.

JIM: Hey, I think that man has (7.) __________ suitcase. See? He probably thinks it's (8.) __________.

BEN: I'll ask him. Excuse me, does this suitcase belong to (9.) __________?

SIMON: Oh, sorry. My mistake! I thought it was (10.) __________!

UNIT 5 FOOD

LESSON A

The Simple Present Tense: Affirmative Statements		
Subject pronoun	**Verb**	
I / You / We / They	eat	meat.
He / She / It	eats	

The Simple Present Tense: Negative Statements					
Subject pronoun	***do***	***not***	**Verb**		**Contractions with *do***
I / You / We / They	**do**	(not)	eat	meat.	do not = don't
He / She / It	**does**				does not = doesn't

Spelling rules for third person singular (*he, she, it*)

In most cases, add *s* to the base form of the verb: *eat* → *eat**s***
If the base form ends in *s, sh, ch, x,* or *z,* add *es*: *teach* → *teach**es***
If the base form ends in consonant + *y*, change the *y* to *i* and add *es*: *study* → *stud**ies***
If the base form ends in consonant + *o*, add *es*: *go* → *go**es*** *do* → *do**es***
The verb *have* is irregular: *have* → ***has***

A Complete the sentences. Use the simple present tense.

1. Maria (live) ___________ in Barcelona, but her parents (live) ___________ in a small town. Of course, she (speak) ___________ Spanish. She also (understand) ___________ some French, but she (not / speak) ___________ it well.
2. Duncan (teach) ___________ at a cooking school. Sarah (go) ___________ to school there, and she (enjoy) ___________ it. School (finish) ___________ at 3:00. After school, Sarah (hurry) ___________ from campus to her part-time job. She (work) ___________ in a restaurant.
3. In my family, we (not / use) ___________ a fork and knife. We (use) ___________ chopsticks to eat our meals. We (have) ___________ rice every day. My little brother (have) ___________ milk every morning. My mother (not / drink) ___________ milk. She (drink) ___________ coffee every morning.

B Rewrite the information in **A** (item 3) above so that it is true for you and your family. Then share it with a partner.

LESSON B

Simple Present *Yes / No* Questions					
do	**Subject**	**Verb**		**Short answers**	**Contractions with *do***
Do	you	like	spicy food?	Yes, I do. / No, I don't.	do not = don't
Does	he / she			Yes, he / she does. / No, he / she doesn't.	does not = doesn't
Do	you			Yes, we do. / No, we don't.	do not = don't
	they			Yes, they do. / No, they don't.	

A Complete the questions and answers.

1. ___Do___ you like spicy food? No, ________________.
2. ______ they speak English? Yes, ________________.
3. ______ he have breakfast every day? No, ________________.
4. ______ we have a test today? Yes, ________________.
5. ______ your mother cook well? Yes, ________________.
6. ______ you and your boyfriend eat lunch together? No, ________________.

B Complete the dialogs with *Yes / No* questions and answers. Then practice with a partner.

1. A: What are you eating?
   B: Pasta with chocolate sauce.
   A: Really? (it / taste) ________________ good?
   B: Yes, ________________. (you / want) ________________ some?
2. A: (you / know) ________________ Jamie Oliver?
   B: No, ________________. Who is he?
   A: He's a famous chef from England.
   B: Oh yeah! (he / have) ________________ a show on TV?
   A: ________________. It's on Channel 4.
3. A: My parents want to go to a nice restaurant. (you / know) ________________ a good place?
   B: (they / like) ________________ spicy food?
   A: Yeah, my dad ________________, but my mom ________________.
   B: Oh, okay. Well, (they / eat) ________________ sushi?
   A: ________________. They love it.
   B: Try Umami Sushi. It's a good place.

C Write short answers to the questions on a piece of paper. Then compare your answers with a partner's.

1. Do you want to try the pasta with chocolate sauce?
2. Do you know Jamie Oliver or other famous chefs?
3. Do your parents like spicy food? How about sushi? Do you?

UNIT 6 RELATIONSHIPS

LESSON A

Possessive Nouns		
Singular nouns (+ 's)	**Plural nouns (+ ')**	**Irregular plural nouns (+ 's)**
sister → sister**'s** brother → brother**'s**	parents → parent**s'** brothers → brother**s'**	children → children**'s** women → women**'s**
For first and last names that end in *s*, you can add **'s** or just **'**.		

A Look up the word *twin* in a dictionary. Read about Hallie Parker and Annie James from the movie *The Parent Trap.* Complete the sentences with a singular noun, a plural noun, or a possessive noun.

1. Hallie Parker lives in her (father) __________ home in California, in the US.
2. Annie (James) __________ home is in London. She lives there with her (mother) __________.
3. The two (girl) __________, Hallie and Annie, are (twin) __________! But they live apart. They don't know about each other.
4. (Hallie) __________ summer plans are exciting. She's going to summer camp. And by chance, (Annie) __________ is going to the same summer camp!
5. At camp, Hallie sees her (sister) __________ face for the first time. They look the same! They are both surprised and happy.
6. Hallie doesn't know her (mom) __________ name, and Annie doesn't know her (dad) __________ name.
7. Before the two (child) __________ leave camp, they have an idea. The two (sister) __________ plan is an exciting one!

B What do you think happens next? Write three sentences. Tell your partner.

____.

____.

____.

LESSON B

Have got			
I'**ve** / You'**ve** / We'**ve** / They'**ve**	**got**	a big family. a nice apartment. a lot of free time. black hair.	**I've got** = I **have got** He**'s got** = He **has got**
He'**s** / She'**s**			

Have got means the same as *have,* but is used in certain situations. You can use *have got* or *have* to talk about relationships, things you own or have, your schedule, or how something looks. It's usually used with the *have* or *has* contracted.

But only use *have* (not *have got*) in these kinds of cases:

I **have** breakfast. (NOT: ~~I've got breakfast...~~)

I **have** fun with my friends. (NOT: ~~I have got fun...~~)

A Complete the sentences with *have got* or *has got*.

1. Paolo isn't single. He ___________ a girlfriend.
2. I ___________ an older sister and a younger brother.
3. Mom isn't home now. She ___________ a doctor's appointment today.
4. My sister and I can't go to the party. We ___________ a lot of homework.
5. Akemi's parents live in Japan. They ___________ a beautiful house there.
6. You ___________ six classes this term? Wow, you're busy!

B Read the sentences. Can you use both *have* and *have got*? Or can you only use *have*? Circle the correct answer(s).

1. A: I have / 've got a question. Is Linda an only child?
   B: No, she has / 's got a brother and sister.
2. A: Do you want something to drink?
   B: Can I have / 've got a glass of water, please?
3. A: Is there a party at Nina's house?
   B: Yes, she has / 's got a party every year for her birthday.
4. A: Is your sister's degree in English?
   B: No, she has / 's got a degree in business.

UNIT 7 TIME

LESSON A

Prepositions of Time		
When is your class?	It's **on** Monday. **on** Mondays. (every Monday) **on** Tuesday night.	day of the week
	It's **in** the morning / afternoon / evening. It's **at** night.	period of the day
	It's **at** 8:30. **at** noon.	specific time
	It's **from** 4:00 **to** 5:30. **from** Tuesday **to** Saturday.	length of time (start to finish)

A Read about Lucia's schedule. Fill in the blanks with *in, on, at, from,* or *to.*

1. My name is Lucia. I'm a nurse. I work ______ Monday ______ Friday.
2. I work in the hospital ______ night. My shift is ______ midnight ______ 9:30 ______ the morning.
3. On workdays, I go to bed ______ 3 PM and wake up ______ 10 PM.
4. I do my grocery shopping ______ the afternoon and ______ Saturdays.
5. It's difficult because my husband works ______ 9 AM ______ 6 PM every day. I don't see him a lot.
6. ______ Sundays, we are both off. We like to go to the park together and relax.

B What do you think of Lucia's schedule? Tell a partner.

C Think of another night job. Answer the questions about the job. Look online to learn more. Then tell a partner.

1. Which days do you work in this job? ____________________
2. What time does the job start and finish? ____________________
3. Is the job easy or difficult? ____________________

LESSON B

Simple Present *Wh-* Questions				
Question word	***do / does***	**Subject**	**Verb**	**Answers**
Who	do	you	study with?	(I study with) Maria.
What	does	she	do on Saturdays?	(She) goes out with friends.
When	do	they	have class?	(They have class) at 8:00.
		we		(We have class) on Mondays.
Where	does	he		(He has class) in Room 3B.

A Read each item. Then use the words in parentheses and information in the responses to complete the questions.

1. A: Who (you) ___do you live___ with?
   B: I live with my sister.
2. A: When (your brother) ______________ in the morning?
   B: He wakes up at 7:15.
3. A: Where (your grandparents) ______________?
   B: They live in London.
4. A: What time (this class) ______________?
   B: It ends at 2:30.
5. A: When (we) ______________ a test in this class?
   B: We have a test tomorrow.
6. A: What (you) ______________ on the weekends?
   B: I go out with my friends.

B Ask a partner the questions in **A**.

UNIT 8 CITY LIFE

LESSON A

Prepositions of Place: *at, on,* and *in*	
A: Where are you? B: I'm **at** school. I'm **on** the second floor, **in** my classroom.	• Use *at* + building: *at the mall, at home* • Use *on* + floor: *on the top floor* • Use *in* + room: *in my office, in the kitchen*
A: Where is it? B: It's **at** 30 Grant Avenue. / It's **on** Grant Avenue.	• Use *at* + address: *at 100 Smith Street* • Use *on* + street: *on Smith Street*

A Complete the conversation with *at*, *on*, *in*, or other prepositions of location from p. 124. Then practice it with a partner.

A: Where are you?

B: I'm still (1.) ________ work!

A: Really? The movie starts in 25 minutes!

B: I know! Where is the theater again?

A: It's (2.) ________ Oak Street. Let's see… it's (3.) ________ 200 Oak Street, to be exact. The theater is (4.) ________ the third floor.

B: OK. Got it. I'm catching a taxi soon.

A: Tell the driver the theater is (5.) ________ to a police station. Let's meet (6.) ________ ________ of the theater.

And after the movie, we can go to the nightclub (7.) ________ from the theater.

B: OK, see you soon!

B Circle the correct words. Complete the sentences with information about yourself.

1. I'm at / on / in school every day from ________ to ________.
2. My classroom is at / on / in the ________ floor.
3. There are a lot of ________ at / on / in my classroom.
4. My school is at / on / in a ________ street.

LESSON B

	Questions and Answers with *How much / How many*	
	Count nouns	**Noncount nouns**
	How many parks are there in your city?	**How much** pollution is there?
Affirmative	(There are) **a lot / many.** **some / a few.** **two.**	(There's) **a lot.** **some / a little.** ----------
Negative	There are**n't many. / Not many.** There are**n't any. / None.**	There is**n't much. / Not much.** There is**n't any. / None.**

How many is used with count nouns. *How much* is used with noncount nouns.
A few means a very small number of something.
It's common to answer *How much / How many* questions with a short answer:
(There are) a lot (of parks). *(There's) a little (pollution).*
The short answers in the negative are *Not many, Not much,* and *None.*

A Circle the best word to complete each sentence.

1. There isn't many / any traffic on the road at the moment.
2. Yesterday, there was a lot of smog, but today, there's only a little / a few.
3. How many / much people live in your neighborhood?
4. A: How many / much rain does this city get in the winter?
   B: It gets a lot / much.

B Complete the dialogs with the words in **bold** in the chart.

1. A: How ______________ bookstores are there in this city?
   B: Not ______________. Most people buy books online now.
2. A: How ______________ traffic is there at 8:30 in the morning?
   B: There's ______________. You can be stuck in traffic for an hour or more.
3. A: How ______________ friends do you have?
   B: ______________. I just moved here. I only know one or two people.
4. A: How ______________ homework do we have tonight?
   B: ______________. The teacher didn't give us any.
5. A: Do you have ______________ free time on the weekend?
   B: I have ______________, about an hour or two.
6. A: How ______________ Thai restaurants are there in your city?
   B: There are ______________. We don't even have one Thai restaurant.

C Now ask and answer the questions in **B** with a partner. Use your own answers.

UNIT 9 ALL ABOUT YOU

LESSON A

Verb + Infinitive	
I **love** to play volleyball. I **forgot** to explain the rules. Can you **learn** to surf in one summer?	The infinitive is *to* + the base form of the verb. It can follow these common verbs: *forget, hate, learn, like, love, need, decide, plan, prepare,* and *want.*

Verb + Noun	
I **like** most sports. I'm **planning** a big trip. We **prepared** dinner for everyone.	All the verbs above can also be followed by a noun or noun phrase.

A Use the verb in parentheses to complete each sentence with the verb + *to* or the verb alone. (Some of the verbs may be in the simple past tense.)

1. I (want) __________ go camping next weekend.
2. Don't (forget) __________ explain the rules.
3. Do you (hate) __________ gym class?
4. I have a silver medal, and now I (want) __________ a gold one.
5. You (need) __________ stretch before you do pilates.
6. I can't go swimming because I (forget) __________ my swimsuit.
7. I'm serious about ping pong. I (hate) __________ lose.
8. I (learn) __________ a new game. Do you want me to show you?

LESSON B

How often...? Frequency Expressions			
How often do you see your best friend?	(I see her)	**every**	day / Monday / week / month / summer.
		once **twice** **three times** **several times**	a day / a week / a month / a year.
		all the time. (= very often) *I see her all the time.* **once in a while.** (= sometimes) *I see her once in a while.* **hardly ever.*** (= almost never) *I hardly ever see her.* **never.** (= not ever)* *I never see her.*	

How often asks about the frequency of an event.

*Frequency expressions usually come at the end of a sentence, but it's more common for *hardly ever* and *never* to come before the verb: *"I **hardly ever** see her." "I **never** see my best friend."*

To say something never happens, you can also say: *Never.*

A Find the mistake in each dialog and correct it. Then practice the dialogs with a partner.

1. A: How often you play tennis?
   B: Every Sunday.
2. A: How often do you wash your hair?
   B: Once a week, on Monday and Friday.
3. A: Is the bus usually on time?
   B: No, it's all the time late.
4. A: How often does Maria see her brother?
   B: Hardly ever she sees him. He works in the UK.

B Look at Ricardo's weekly schedule. Answer the questions with a word or phrase in **bold** in the chart.

Monday	Tuesday	Wednesday	Thursday	Friday	Saturday	Sunday
Class: 9–12 Work: 1–4	Work: 10–2	Class: 9–12 Work: 1–4	Work: 10–2	Class: 9–12 Work: 1–4	Study group: 10–12 Work: 1–4	Work: 3–6

How often does Ricardo...	Answer
1. have class?	1a. once a week.
	1b. on Monday, Wednesday, and Friday.
2. work?	2a. ________ day.
	2b. ________ time.
3. work from 10 to 2?	3a. ________ a week.
	3b. ________ Tuesday and Thursday.
4. work from 1 to 4?	4a. ________ a week.
	4b. ________ Monday, Wednesday, Friday, and Saturday.
5. meet with his study group?	5a. ________.
	5b. ________.

UNIT 10 HEALTH

LESSON A

Affirmative and Negative Forms of the Imperative

Don't	Base form	
	Stay	calm.
Don't	panic.	
	Go	to the airport.
Don't	leave	without your passport.
	Take	two aspirin daily.
Don't	forget	to take your medicine.

Use the imperative to give advice, instructions, directions, and orders.

Add *please* to make orders and requests more polite: *Please don't smoke here. Move outside, please.*

A Complete each item with the correct answer. Then compare your answers with a partner.

1. I feel sick. Please take ________.
   a. me to the doctor　　b. some medicine
2. We're leaving for the airport. Don't ________ your passport.
   a. bring　　b. forget
3. Shh! ________ quiet. ________ any noise.
   a. Don't be; Make　　b. Be; Don't make
4. Does your eye hurt? Don't ________!
   a. rub it　　b. put in eye drops
5. ________ the instructions again, please. I couldn't hear you the first time.
   a. Read　　b. Don't read
6. It says, "Be careful! ________ this medicine on an empty stomach."
   a. Bring　　b. Don't take

LESSON B

When Clauses	
***When* clause**	**Result clause**
When(ever) I drink coffee,	I can't sleep.
Result clause	***When* clause**
I can't sleep	when(ever) I drink coffee.

These sentences talk about things that are usually true: When *X* happens, *Y* is the result.
The present tense is used in the *when* clause and the result clause.
The result clause can come first or second in a sentence. When it comes first, there is no comma between the result clause and the *when* clause.

A Match a *when* clause on the left with a result clause on the right to make sentences.

1. When I feel stressed,
2. When we argue,
3. When I sleep well,
4. When I don't eat breakfast,
5. When you're kind,
6. When I miss the bus,

a. people are usually nice to you.
b. I get hungry by 10:00.
c. my mom usually apologizes first.
d. I exercise.
e. I'm late for class.
f. I have a lot of energy.

B Rewrite the sentences in **A** so that the result comes first. Then tell your partner which sentences are true for you. Explain your answers.

1. I exercise when I feel stressed.
2. ______.
3. ______.
4. ______.
5. ______.
6. ______.

C Compare your answers in **B** with a different partner.

I exercise when I feel stressed.

Really? I don't.

UNIT 11 JOBS

LESSON A

Questions with *like*	
A: My mom works in a hospital. B: Really? **What's** that **like**? A: It's hard, but she enjoys it.	You can use *like* to ask questions about an experience. In this question, *that* = *working in a hospital.*
A: My coworker is from Brazil. B: Oh? **What's** he **like**? A: He's really nice / friendly / outgoing / smart.	You can also use *like* to ask questions about a person and his or her personality. *What's (he) like?* *What are (they) like?*

A Complete the dialogs with the correct questions.

1. A: Ms. Collins is my math teacher this term.
   B: Oh? ______
   A: She's really nice.
2. A: I'm a student at Stanford University.
   B: Really? ______
   A: It's a great school. I love it.
3. A: My brother works in an office.
   B: ______
   A: Sometimes it's boring, but he likes it.
4. A: My tutor is from London.
   B: Really? ______
   A: He's very friendly.

LESSON B

Talking about Ability with *can / can't*		
I / You / He / She / We / They	**can / can't**	speak French.

Can and *can't* are followed by the base form of the verb.
Can't is the short form of *cannot*. In spoken English, *can't* is more common.

Questions with *can / can't*		
***Yes / No* questions**	**Can** you speak Spanish?	Yes, I **can**. / No, I **can't**.
***Wh-* questions**	Which languages **can** Carla speak?	(She **can** speak) Spanish and English.
	Who **can** speak Japanese?	Toshi (**can**).

A Complete the dialogs with a question or answer with *can* or *can't*.

1. A: Can Mario drive?
   B: No, ________. He's only 14.
2. A: ____________________?
   B: Yes, I can. I'm a good driver.
3. A: ____________________?
   B: No, Jun's parents can't speak English.
4. A: ____________________?
   B: Yes, Linda can swim, but her sister ________.

B Make questions and answers about Adam and Sonya using *can* and the words given.

Adam:	musician	**Sonya:**	programmer
Languages:	English and Chinese	**Languages:**	Spanish and English
Hobbies:	I like to ski and play guitar.	**Hobbies:**	I like to dance and ski.

1. Who / speak Chinese? ____________________
   Adam can speak Chinese.
2. What / languages / Sonya / speak? ____________________
   ____
3. Who / build / websites? ____________________
   ____
4. What / instrument / Adam / play? ____________________
   ____
5. Who / ski? ____________________
   ____

C Ask and answer the questions in **A** and **B** aloud with a partner.

UNIT 12 AT THE MOVIES

LESSON A

The Present Continuous as Future			
Subject + *be*	**Verb + *ing***		**Future time expression**
We're	seeing	a movie	today / tonight / tomorrow. in an hour. this weekend.
They're	making		next year.

You can use the present continuous tense (often with a future time expression) to talk about future plans.

Use the present continuous only when a plan exists:

Here's the plan: We're meeting downtown and then driving to the theater in my car.

Do not use the present continuous to make predictions. Use *going to* instead:

~~*He's passing the test tomorrow.*~~ *He's going to pass the test tomorrow.*

A Complete the conversation. Use the present continuous form of the verbs in parentheses and complete the time expression with the words in the box.

in	next	this	tomorrow

A: I'm really looking forward to summer vacation (1.) ____this____ year.

B: Why is that?

A: Because (2. I / go) ____________ to Tanzania, in Africa. (3. we / leave) ____________ (4.) ____________ morning! I'm so excited!

B: Wow! How (5. you / get) ____________ there?

A: (6. we / fly) ____________ with Global Airways from New York City. And (7. we / change) ____________ planes in Dubai before arriving in Dar es Salaam.

B: Do you already have a plan for the trip?

A: Yes, (8. we / visit) ____________ Zanzibar for a few days and then (9. climb) ____________ Mount Kilimanjaro.

B: Great! How long is the trip?

A: (10. I / stay) ____________ for two weeks, so (11. I / return) ____________ early (12.) ____________ month. (13. my friend / travel) ____________ an extra week in Africa. What about you? (14. you / go) ____________ anywhere fun?

B: Not really. (15. I / visit) ____________ my family down south. (16. I / drive) ____________ and (17. I / leave) ____________ (18.) ____________ a few hours.

i Verbs that are related to movement and travel (like *go, come, take, fly, travel, visit, leave, arrive,* and *get*) are commonly used in the present continuous when expressing future time.

LESSON B

-ed Adjectives	*-ing* Adjectives
1a. I'm **bored**. I don't like this movie.	**1b**. This movie is **boring**. Let's watch something else.
2a. I was **surprised** by the ending.	**2b**. The end of the movie was **surprising**.

Use *-ed* adjectives to describe a person's feelings. For example, in sentence 1a, you can say *I'm bored*, (meaning "I feel bored") but not ~~*I'm boring*~~.

Use *-ing* adjectives to describe a situation, an activity, or person that makes you feel a certain way: *That movie was boring. My math teacher is very inspiring.*

Here are some common *-ed* / *-ing* adjectives. Review their meanings with your instructor and classmates.

amazed / amazing	embarrassed / embarrassing	interested / interesting
bored / boring	entertained / entertaining	relaxed / relaxing
confused / confusing	excited / exciting	shocked / shocking
depressed / depressing	frightened / frightening	surprised / surprising
disappointed / disappointing	inspired / inspiring	terrified / terrifying

A Complete the movie review. Circle the correct words. Did Paula like the movie?

Actor Sean Clarkson is in the new sci-fi thriller *Midnight on the Moon*. Overall, I was very disappointed / disappointing with this film. Some scenes in the film are excited / exciting, and newcomer Kristin Cox is interested / interesting as Clarkson's love interest in the movie. But the story is often confused / confusing. I didn't understand the ending at all. I was also surprised / surprising by some scenes in the film. They were very violent!

B Complete the sentences with the correct form of the words in the box.

bore	confuse	depress	embarrass	entertain	surprise	terrify

1. I was kind of ____________ after watching that movie. It was a tearjerker!
2. I'm ____________. Is our test this Friday or next Friday?
3. My film class is very ____________. It's a lot of fun.
4. I watched a scary movie alone, and I was ____________. It was very frightening!
5. When that movie won Best Film, it was ____________. In my opinion, it was a terrible movie.
6. This movie is very ____________—not interesting at all.
7. I fell asleep during class, and the teacher yelled at me. How ____________!

Answer Key

Answers to page 147, Communication: Personality Quiz, Exercise B

Green	Blue	Purple	Orange
You're generous and you care about other people. You want to help them. But sometimes, you're too picky! Remember, people aren't perfect.	You're ambitious and a little bit reserved. But remember—it's important to smile. Don't be so serious all the time!	You love to learn and try new things. You're also very bright. But sometimes, you're too competitive. Let others win once in a while!	You're interesting, and you love adventure. But be careful! Sometimes you're very impulsive! Remember to think about your future, too!

Photo Credits

2-3 Courtesy of Manuel Paz Castanal; **4** Danilda Izquierdo; **5** (tl) Dream Pictures/Blend/Corbis, (tr) Celso Diniz/Shutterstock.com, (ct) naka-stockphoto/Shutterstock.com, (cb) El Nariz/Shutterstock.com; **6** (t) Niar/Shutterstock.com, (tr) Kichigin/Shutterstock.com; **7** Yellow Dog Productions/The Image Bank/Getty Images; **9** (b) iStockphoto.com/leminuit; **12–13** Lloyd Bishop/NBC/NBCU Photo Bank via Getty Images, (b) Tristan Fewings/Getty Images; **15** (tl) Dmitry_Tsvetkov/Shutterstock.com, (tr) Ammentorp Photography/Shutterstock.com, (cl) Hero Images/Getty Images, (cr) Goodluz/Shutterstock.com; **18-19** (spread) Brian Yen; **20** (t) Henrik Sorensen/Getty Images; **21** (cr) StockRocket/Getty Images, (bc) Antoniodiaz/Shutterstock.com, (bl) Carlina Teteris/Getty Images, (c) Images by Tang Ming Tung/Getty Images, (cl) Tara Moore/Getty Images, (cr) Whitetag/Getty Images, (cl) Chris Schmidt/Getty Images, (c) Mustafa Arican/Getty Images; **22-23** (spread) ©Alex Treadway/National Geographic Creative; **25** (b) Image Source/Getty Images; 56 (t) Carlos Cazalis/Corbis News/Corbis; **27** (tl) Philipp igumnov flickr. com/photos/woodcum/Getty Images, (tr) Erik Isakson/Getty Image, (cr) Vitchanan Photography/Shutterstock.com; **28-29** (spread) Ian Trower/Passage/Corbis; **29** (cr) ImageRite/Alamy; **30** (t) Izabela Habur/Getty Images; **34-35** Alessio Mamo/Redux; **36** Karine Aigner/NGC, **39** Cultura RM/Gu/Getty Images; **41** Michael Melford/NGC; **42** Kirill_Liv/Getty Images; **43** (tl) Anna Bryukhanova/iStockphoto.com, (tl) Brent Lewin/Bloomberg/Getty Images, (tr) View Pictures/Getty Images, (tr) Anton Gvozdikov/Shutterstock.com; **44-45** Massimo Borchi/Terra/Corbis; **52-53** Sebastian Walhuetter, **54** Emanuele Siracusa/NGC; **55** Steve Winter/NGC; **56** Michael Reusse/Westend61/Corbis; **57** Radoslaw Lecyk/Shutterstock.com; **58** Somyot Chamnanrith/NGC; **59** (tl) IakovKalinin/Getty Images, (tc) Samot/Shutterstock.com, (tr) Nisa and Ulli Maier Photography/Moment/Getty Images, (cl) Olga Danylenko/Shutterstock.com, (c) EpicStockMedia/Shutterstock.com, (cr) maxpro/Shutterstock.com, (bl) Don Bayley/istockphoto.com, (bc) photostogo.com, (br) Keren Su/Getty Images; **60** (tl) axstokes/Getty Images, (tl) Jupiterimages/Getty Images/Comstock/Thinkstock.com, (tr) Frank and Helena/Getty Images, (tr) Roberto Westbrook/Getty Images, (bl) CJG - Technology/Alamy, (bl) StockLite/Shutterstock.com, (br) Halfdark/Getty Images, (br) conejota/Shutterstock.com; **61** (tl) SunKids/Shutterstock.com, (tr) Jason Homa/Getty Images, (cl) Stockbyte/Getty Images, (cr) Jupiterimages/Photos.com; **62-63** Steve Raymer/NGC; **65** (tr) Thomas Wasserberg/Getty Images, (tl) suttisukmek/Getty Images, (tl) amanaimagesRF/Getty Images, (tl) Bill Noll/Getty Images; **68-69** (spread) Penny do los Santos; **70** (t) Andrew Aitchison/Alamy; **71** (c) spaxiax/Shutterstock.com, (cl) Michael Gray/Getty Images, (bc) Brent Hofacker/Shutterstock.com, (c) Sally Scott/Getty Images, (bl) Darryl rooks/Shutterstock. com, (cl) Olga Nayashkova/Shutterstock.com, (cr) VeselovaElena/Getty Images, (cr) OlgaMiltsova/Getty Images; **73** (tr) Igor Dutina/Shutterstock.com; **74** (b) ViewStock/Getty Images; 69 (tc) Geo Martinez/Shutterstock.com, (cr) Paul Bradbury/Getty Images, (c) Sam Edwards/Getty Images, (tr) blackdovfx/Getty Image, (tl) Tara Moore/Getty Images, (cl) Nicholas Monu/Getty Images; **76** (t) MATTHIEU PALEY/National Geographic Creative; **77** (cl) craftvision/Getty Images, (tl) DonNichols/Getty Images, (cl) Edward Westmacott/Shutterstock.com, (tc) kai keisuke/Shutterstock.com, (tc) Foodcollection RF/Getty Images, (c) obewon/Getty Images, (tr) Nikolai Pozdeev /Shutterstock.com, (cr) Crisp/Shutterstock.com; **78-79** (spread) Bruno Ehrs/Latitude/Corbis; **79** (br) Domenico Tondini/Alamy; **80** (b) ©Robert Clark/National Geographic Creative; **81** (c) Dave G Kelly/Getty Images; **84-85** (spread) Chris de Bruyn; **86** (t) National Geographic Channels; **87** (tl) Fuse/Getty Image, (bl) Air Images/Shutterstock.com, (cl) Carlos Hernandez/STOCK4B-RF/Getty Images, (bc) Valua Vitaly/Shutterstock.com, (cr) Dimitri Otis/Getty Images, (cr) oliveromg/Shutterstock.com, (bl) Mat Hayward/Shutterstock.com, (br) JuliaLine/Shutterstock.com, (tr) Pali Rao/Getty Images, (cl) Morsa Images/Getty Images; **88** (tl) Jupiterimages/Getty Images; **89** (t) Yellow Dog Productions/Taxi/Getty Images; **91** (t) Mark Cuthbert/Getty Images; **93** (b) Michael Dwyer/Alamy; **94-95** (spread) ©Guillaume Herbaut/INSTITUTE; **96** (b) 2 Image Source/Ocean/Corbis; **102-103** (spread) Interpixels/Shutterstock.com; **104** (t) ©David Evans/National Geographic creative; **107** (tr) Peter Beavis/Getty Images; **108** (cr) Dave G.Houser/Alamy; **109** (t) Jon Hicks/Latitude/Corbis; **110** (t) ©Paul Nicklen/National Geographic Creative; **111** (b) Arena Creative/Shutterstock.com; **112-113** (spread) Kamil Tamiola/Aurora Photos; **113** (br) DreamPictures/Getty Images, (bl) Jupiterimages/Getty Images, (bc) B Busco/Getty Images; **118-119** (spread) Interpixels/Shutterstock.com; **120** (t) ©David Evans/National Geographic creative; **123** (tr) Peter Beavis/Getty Images; **124** (cr) Dave G. Houser/Alamy; **125** (t) Jon Hicks/Latitude/Corbis; **126** (t) ©Paul Nicklen/National Geographic Creative; **127** (b) Arena Creative/Shutterstock. com; **128-129** (spread) Kamil Tamiola/Aurora Photos; **129** (br) DreamPictures/Getty Images, (bl) Jupiterimages/Getty Images, (bc) B Busco/Getty Images; **134-135** Courtesy of Sash Fitzsimmons; **136** (t) Charley Gallay/Getty Images; **137** (bc) ©IM_photo/Shutterstock. com, (bc) ©GaudiLab/Shutterstock.com, (bl) STR/Getty Images, (br) ©Andrey Popov/Shutterstock.com, (c) ©Pedro Monteiro/Shutterstock.com, (c) ©Kaderov Andrii/Shutterstock.com, (c) ©EpicStockMedia/Shutterstock.com, (c) ©Mindscape studio/Shutterstock.com, (cl) Brocreative/Shutterstock.com, (cl) ©dotshock/Shutterstock.com, (cr) Nate Jordan/Aflo Foto Agency Royalty Free/AGE Fotostock, (tc) ©EpicStockMedia/Shutterstock.com, (tc) ©GaudiLab/Shutterstock.com, (tl) ©David Lee/Shutterstock.com, (tr) ©muzsy/Shutterstock.com, (tr) isitsharp/istock/Getty images; **138** (b) ©EpicStockMedia/Shutterstock.com; **141** (bl) Mike Hewitt - FIFA/Getty Images; **142** (tl) ©Creativa Images/Shutterstock.com, (tr) ©takayuki/Shutterstock.com; **143** (cl) ©Helder Almeida/Shutterstock.com, (cr) digitalskillet/iStock\Getty Images; **144-145** Eric Tschaen/REA/Redux Eric Tschaen/REA/Redux; **145** (cr) ©s_bukley/Shutterstock.com, (tr) The Asahi Shimbun/Getty Images, (tr) DESIREE MARTIN/Getty Images; **147** (tr) ©James Woodson/Digital Vision/Getty Images RF; **152-153** Tim Kemple; **154** (t) Courtesy of Dr_Ellsworth_Wareham; **155** (t) MIKE STURK/Corbis Wire/Corbis; **156** (tr) Ricardo Reitmeyer/Shutterstock; **158** (br) RICH REID/National Geographic Creative; **160** (tl) Prasit photo/Getty Images, (tr) ©Syda Productions/Shutterstock.com; **161** (tl) powerofforever/iStockphoto.com, (tc) ©Wutthichai/Shutterstock.com, (c) Hemis/Maisant Ludovic/hemis.fr/Alamy, (tr) Ian Dagnall/Alamy; **162-163** Peter Macdiarmid/Getty Images; **165** (br) Monkey Business Images/Shutterstock.com; **168-169** (spread) Kyle Kurlick; **170** (t) ©Skip Brown/National Geographic Creative; **171** (tc) Wavebreakmedia/Shutterstock.com, (cl) iStockphoto.com/Aleksey_Panov, (br) Minerva Studio/Shutterstock.com, (tl) Comstock Images/Getty Images, (bc) Chinaview/Shutterstock.com, (tc) Net Magazine/Getty Images, (cr) Gpointstudio/Getty Images, (bl) Paul Bradbury/Getty Images, (c) Image Source/Getty Images, (c) Junial Enterprises/Shutterstock.com, (bc) Sean Locke Photography/Shutterstock.com, (tr) Monkey Business Images/Shutterstock.com; **172** (tr) Hero Images Inc/Hero Images/Corbis; **174** (b) Douglas Graham/Getty Images; **176** (t) Tasos Katopodis/Getty Images; **177** (tl) Yoshikazu Tsuno/Getty Images, (tr) Blackregis/Shutterstock.com; **178-179** (spread) Clodagh Kilcoyne/Getty Images; **179** (b) Kirsten Luce/The New York Times/Redux; **180** (c) Jill Gocher/Asia Images/Getty Images; **184-185** LYNSEY ADDARIO/National Geographic Creative; **186** (t) Arin Sang-Urai; **187** (cl) Lionsgate/Everett Collection, (cr) Film Fanatique/Alamy, (tr) 2013 Warner Bros Entertainment Inc/RatPac Entertainment/DR/Photoshot, (bl) AF archive/Alamy, (bc) Everett Collection/Alamy, (br) Photos 12/Alamy; **188** (b) Natalie Cass/Getty Images; **189** (tr) Sean Pavone/Shutterstock.com; **190** (bl) Ethan Miller/Getty Images; **191** (bl) Movie Poster Image Art/Getty Images; **192** (t) DreamPictures/Getty Images; **193** (tr) Guy Spangenberg/Passage/Corbis; **194-195** Pietus/Shutterstock.com; **195** (tr) AF archive/Alamy, (tl) AF archive/Alamy; **197** (t) Hubert Stadler/Documentary Value/Corbis; **200** (tl) Minerva Studio/Shutterstock.com, (tr) Photon-Photos/Getty Images, (cb) Scott Cramer/Getty Images